A Garland Series

The
Life & Times
of
Seven Major British Writers

Dryden
Pope
Swift
Richardson
Sterne
Johnson
Gibbon

*A collection of 370 titles printed
in photo-facsimile in 147 volumes*

A Reply
to the
Reasonings of Mr. Gibbon
1778

by
Smyth Loftus

Garland Publishing, Inc., New York & London

1974

Bibliographical note:

this facsimile has been made from a copy in the
Cornell University Library
(Rare DG.311.G44L82. 1778)

Library of Congress Cataloging in Publication Data

Loftus, Smyth.
    A reply to the reasonings of Mr. Gibbon.

    (The life & times of seven major British writers.
Gibboniana, 3)
    Reprint of the 1778 ed. printed in Dublin.
    1. Gibbon, Edward, 1737-1794. The history of the
decline and fall of the Roman empire. 2. Apologetics--
18th century. I. Gibbon, Edward, 1737-1794. The
history of the decline and fall of the Roman empire.
II. Title. III. Series: Gibboniana, 3.
DG206.G5G52 vol. 3 [DG311] 937'.06'072024s
ISBN 0-8240-1340-9   [937'.06'072024] 74-18385

75-2399
Printed in the United States of America

A

R E P L Y

TO THE

Reasonings of Mr. *Gibbon*.

[Price 2s. 6d.]

A

R E P L Y

TO THE

REASONINGS OF MR. GIBBON,

IN HIS

HISTORY of the DECLINE and FALL

OF THE

ROMAN EMPIRE,

Which feem to affect the TRUTH of CHRIS-
TIANITY, but have not been noticed in the
ANSWER which Dr. WATSON hath given to
that Book.

By SMYTH LOFTUS, M.A.
Vicar of COOLOCK, in IRELAND.

~~~~~~

Pafs over the Ifles of Chittim, and fee; and fend unto
Kidor, and confider diligently, and fee if there be
fuch a Thing. Hath a Nation changed their Gods,
which yet are no Gods? But my People have changed
their Glory, for that which doth not profit.

~~~~~~

D U B L I N, printed:
LONDON, reprinted for J. WILLIAMS, in Fleet-
Street; and J. BEW, in Pater-Nofter-Row.
MDCCLXXVIII.

A

R E P L Y

TO THE

REASONINGS OF Mr. GIBBON,
&c.

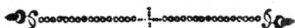

CHAPTER I.

MY firm belief of that religion which diftinguifhes its author and itfelf by a commandment to " love one another," and confequently to promote, to the utmoft of our power, the happinefs of all mankind, and more efpecially of all our fellow-chriftians, hath induced me to attempt a defence of it againft the attacks

B   of

of the more ingenious than candid Mr. Gibbon, who, in his History of the Decline of the Roman Empire, has endeavoured totally to deftroy it, and to introduce I know not what, it is more than probable he himfelf knows not what, in the place of it; but this I can tell him, he would introduce fuch a profligacy of principle and manners, as muft totally difqualify the reader, with whom he has any fuccefs, for any happinefs either in this or the next world ; and that, whether confidered as an individual, or a member of fociety, the providence of God, and the nature of man, both of them unite to bear me out in this affertion.

I look upon it as a fortunate incident for Ireland, that Dr. Watfon's Anfwer came out here almoft as foon as Mr. Gibbon's

Gibbon's book ; for it confutes the moſt
difficult and pernicious parts of it. But
as this gentleman hath ſtudied conciſeneſs
ſo much as to omit many things which
to the leſs knowing reader may want an
explanation, I have endeavoured to remedy this defect, by writing theſe obſer-
vations, which will give a tolerable view
of the whole controverſy, and extend to
thoſe objections againſt chriſtianity, which
are the great foundations of our modern
unbelief.

One ſhould imagine, that deiſtical writers, who all declare for a religion of
Nature, and this ſo perfect, that nothing
can be added to or diminiſhed from it,
and the whole of it likewiſe ſo certain
and manifeſt that no inſtruction can be
wanted or given in it even by God himſelf :—one ſhould imagine, at leaſt, that
theſe

these gentlemen would confer some honour upon christianity, not only for
teaching a much more perfect and beneficial morality, and enforcing it by infinitely more powerful motives, than had
ever been known by mankind before;
but likewise for its furnishing us with a
perfect knowledge of God, his laws,
nature, government, and true religion,
and the pure worship with which he is
to be served; which knowledge must be
most advantageous to virtue and the happiness of mankind, and thereby preserve
them from that abominable superstition
of the heathens which must prove so
pernicious to both :—one should imagine
that this absurd and idolatrous paganism
should be as severely, as it would be
most justly, condemned by those setters-
up of religion, and christianity in the
same manner approved of and commended

mended by them. But nothing like this, nay, the very reverfe of this, is to be found in all our infidel writings.

The great genius and learning of Mr. Gibbon, and his acquaintance with the heathen and primitive chriftian writers, muft have informed him, that the groffeft immorality was not only permitted but required by the Gentile religion ; that their gods, nay the very chief of them, were made up of the undutiful and inceftuous, of the abufers of themfelves with mankind, of the favage and murderer, of the thief and cheat. He cannot be ignorant that they confeffedly worfhipped evil beings to prevent their doing them mifchief ; that human facrifices were univerfal among them ; that they were practifed even in their moft civilized nations, and frequently offered up with an excefs

B 3 of

of cruelty and torture. He must know that many of their religious services did require drunkenness, lewdness, pollution, blood, murder, even to their burning to ashes their own living children, and sometimes in great numbers, of their most noble and best families, to their horrible and malicious idols and devils: for nothing but such accursed spirits could have inspired or been pleased with such a service as this.

With all these things must Mr. Gibbon be well acquainted, and must likewise know that all their wise philosophers were so ignorant or timorous in these matters, that they all, outwardly, conformed to the religions of their several countries, and advised all others to do the same; and when christianity arose, instead of abandoning this detestable superstition,

perſtition, did, generally, endeavour to defend it ; and, therefore, with equal falſehood and malice, did miſrepreſent chriſtianity, and abuſe it as the baſeſt and moſt abominable of all falſe and bad religions. He cannot be, he is not, ignorant of their abſurd notions of a future life, and the retributions of it ; but makes their very honeſt philoſophers, and the prieſts themſelves, deride the whole of their religious ſervices, whilſt they officiated in them. What a charming religion of nature was this, and what worthy guides in it were their philoſophers and great men, upon whoſe integrity Mr. Gibbon, in other places, can himſelf repoſe, and would have others likewiſe repoſe, ſuch an unlimited confidence.

Thus abominably falſe was the pagan religion ; and what a ſad effect muſt this

have

have had upon the morals of the people, when they were, even by their religion, initiated into wickedneſs; and muſt, be-ſides, be naturally led to imitate the ac-tions of theſe gods whom they worſhip-ped and thought it their duty to pleaſe ? Theſe were their gods, and ſuch their worſhip, whilſt the one true God was totally abandoned by them; and yet Mr. Gibbon, in page 553 of his firſt vo-lume, inſtead of condemning, ſeems ra-ther to praiſe this perverſion of all reli-gion. The folly and falſehood of it are, indeed, acknowledged; but its unclean-neſs, madneſs, violence, cruelty, are all kept out of ſight, and this monſtrous ſuperſtition treated by him rather as an innocent and uſeful, than a moſt crimi-nal and pernicious deceit; and an occa-ſion taken to commend it for its mild-neſs and toleration; although it would

bear

bear no religion but fuch as was founded upon its own bottom, nor fometimes all of this neither; and though it fhewed itfelf fo cruel and bloody to the beft of mankind for profeffing chriftianity, and refufing to join in this their abominable idolatry.

CHAP.

CHAP. II.

HAVING, with the primitive christian apologists, concisely shewn what that heathenism was which Mr. Gibbon so undeservedly spares, or rather commends, let us with them turn to christianity, and see, likewise, what this religion is which he so unmeritedly condemns, and is endeavouring to destroy.

Christianity informs us that there is one infinite, eternal, all-powerful, omniscient Spirit, whom we call God; who, as he is absolutely perfect in his being, and the producer of all other beings, so likewise in morality or holiness; for he is infinitely pure, just, merciful, good, and true, and therefore the greatest lover

possible

possible of virtue, and hater of vice. It tells us that the heavens and the earth, and all things in them, were created, do subsist, and are governed by him :—that he was too good to make man for this insignificant life alone, but hath formed him for an endless and perfect existence in a new life, and an everlasting and inconceivable glory and happiness in it, provided he will, by proper behaviour in this world, qualify or make himself capable of them :—that the qualification required, is for him so to act in this present life as shall render him the most lovely and happy being in himself, most beneficial to every creature with whom he is connected, and to whom his influence can extend, and as shall fill him with those affections which will assimilate him to the all-perfect God, and train his heart to the enjoyment of that being

Being in whom alone the perfect happinefs of all intelligent creatures is to be
found, and upon a likenefs to whom it
muft for ever depend.

Chriftianity tells us, that weak, fallen,
and finful as all men are, and perfectly
holy and juft as their God, yet he is not
man's enemy, but his moft affectionate
and beneficent friend; for even to us
finners God is love :—that he does not
defert us as foon as he has made us, but
watches continually over us to do us
good, and this with fuch a particular
providence, that a hair falls not from our
heads but with his knowledge and by
his permiffion :—that we may, in every
cafe, addrefs ourfelves to him in prayer,
for protection, deliverance, guidance,
bleffing, and be fure of obtaining them
all, fo far as they are good for us ; provided.

vided we intreat them with fit difpofitions, and in the proper manner which he hath prefcribed to us ; and from hence fhews us we have a certainty, that, with our own honeft endeavours, he will carry us fafe through all our dangers here, whether of life or death, and never quit our protection till he has lodged us for ever fafe in heaven and its inconceivable blifs. What glorious and happy privileges are thefe for men ! But chriftianity tells us, that this is a bleffed condition, to which we are not of ourfelves entitled, but which has been moft dearly purchafed for us by our redemption in Chrift.

For inafmuch as all men are finners, and the great Creator and Governor of the univerfe is of fuch a nature as to hold all finners in abhorrence, and he muft likewife, as he values the happinefs of

his

his whole creation, diffuade by the moſt powerful motives poſſible from all ſin, and perfuade to virtue ; therefore has the moſt perfectly juſt and holy, but moſt merciful and loving God, contrived a way to ſave man, which ſhall the beſt anſwer to both theſe purpoſes, at the ſame time that it procures pardon, fa-vour, and happineſs for man, the ſinner. For to ſave mankind from the deſtructive nature and horrible effect of ſin, did that Son of God, who is himſelf the efficient and final cauſe and fuſtainer of all things, become man, with all the innocent weakneſs and infirmities of this low nature, that, by therein performing for us the whole will of God, without any ſin, he might cloath us with his own righteouſneſs ; and, by dying in all the tortures of the croſs for us, he might ex-piate our ſins, and reconcile us to his

all-

all-holy father, and our offended God.
By all thefe providences have we the
greateſt deteſtation poſſible ſhewn to ſin,
and yet love to his creatures though ſinners: and nothing could ever ſo affect-
ingly prove the dreadfully odious and
pernicious nature of vice, and the abſolute neceſſity of virtue in order to our
future happineſs, as does this chriſtian
ſcheme of ſalvation. And, to encreaſe
this conviction, we are not yet, with all
this exceſs of kindneſs manifeſted to us,
permitted to put up a petition to him
but through the mediation of this infi-
nitely-deſerving Redeemer; nor are we
capable of any acceptance from him,
but through the fanctification of his all-
powerful and Holy Spirit, who ſhall new
create our fallen and corrupted nature,
and thereby render us capable of that
divine favour and happineſs for which

we

we were at first created. And thus is
the whole of our salvation from our God,
who himself atones, sanctifies, pardons,
blesses, and is all in all to the true christian. Besides, to give us an undoubted
assurance of his having obtained all these
blessings for us, he rises from the grave
and conquers death, the penalty of sin,
ascends into heaven, the place of our
happiness, to take possession before-hand
for us; he is invested with all power,
both in heaven and earth; he visibly
sends down from thence the gifts of his
Holy Spirit upon men: and because he
loved us to such an inconceivable degree,
therefore is he appointed the judge of
all creatures, and he himself it is who is
to award them all to their proper fate,
whether of happiness or misery, for ever;
and our salvation put entirely into his
power.

By

By these means have we the most certain and comfortable assurance of our
being all saved upon the easy terms
of the Gospel, and made partakers of
endless life and inconceivable happiness.
And shall any man wilfully cast away
these blessings from him? It is true that
they are most wonderful; and, where
a wrong bias of mind hath been contracted, that they will appear hard of
belief, or utterly incredible. But, to take
off this incredibility, let it be confidered,
that God is an infinite being, and must
therefore be exalted as much above men
in his workings, as in his incomprehen-
fible nature; and as every person acquainted with his material creation, must
acknowledge, that he is here inscrutable
where yet there can be no oppofition
made to his will, fo must he be much
more inscrutable in the formation and

C   govern-

government of his moral creatures, who to be moral muſt be free, and therefore governed according to their freedom ; but who, if they be free, will many of them, for preſent gratification, be ever flying off from that rule of right to which all happineſs is, and muſt be, annexed, and thereby introducing evil, inſtead of the Creator's intended good, into his good creation. Where this happens to be the caſe, a remedy will be manifeſtly wanted; and certainly it is ſo in this our world : and we find that the divine power, wiſdom, goodneſs, are greatly, I had almoſt ſaid principally, here diſplayed, by the very many and various remedies which he hath provided for the numberleſs evils which immorality and wickedneſs have introduced into our world, and to which we are here ſo miſerably ſubjected.

Beſides

Befides, the divine Being muft ever be diftinguifhed and glorified by his work-ings, and chiefly, no doubt, by his work-ings to do good ; and, if fo, it muft be by providences of mercy and kindnefs which fhall be expreffive of his infinity, and therefore ftupendous and wonderful beyond all created conception. And if it be confidered, that a love to virtue and his creatures muft ever be the higheft affections in the divine mind, and muft, by the manifeftations which he fhall here-in make of his nature, do the moft ho-nour to himfelf and benefit to all moral beings ; (for this will beget in them the greateft love to, and happinefs in him, and fill them with thefe affections which are of all others the moft lovely and blifsful ;) we fhall then fee abundant rea-fon for this providence of Chriftianity, and in fullnefs of conviction acknow-

C 2   ledge,

ledge, that he hath hereby deservedly gotten himself a name which is above every name that ever was or shall be named, whether in heaven or earth, whether in this world or in the world to come; and does most peculiarly merit the most thankful and high adoration and praise of every creature, upon account of this wonderful work of our redemption in Christ.

But it will be asked, Is this, indeed, the whole of Christianity? I answer that it is not; for this religion is made up of threatenings as well as of promises; and denounces a Hell of never-ending torments to the wicked, as well as it engages a Heaven of the like happiness to the virtuous person :—a declaration this, truly affecting and awful to the most virtuous of men; but, to the many

wicked

wicked among us, fo horrible, that it
muft make them wifh, and eagerly too,
that death may be to them, what it is
now frequently ·ftyled, the end of all
exiftence. But who are they with whom
this muft be the cafe ? Why only with
thofe· men who will facrifice the boafted
dignity of rational and moral man, to
the low appetites and paffions of irrational and immoral brute. And where
this is the caufe of infidelity to any, how
very bafe and deteftable muft the infidel
be ? Every animal is made to defire enjoyment ; and man, by knowing that
there can be no enjoyment without exiftence, is made to defire exiftence, and
this without end : and herein· his animal
nature joins in with his reafon ; for it
makes him abhor, and, to the utmoft of
his power, to refift and ftrive againft
death and an extinction of being. And

C 3.   what

what is it, then, which can cause these
people to wish for this extinction? Why
it is, that they may here wallow in all
sensuality without any thought or care of
religion or futurity, and yet avoid that
wounded conscience which would make
them justly apprehend, that, if there
should be another life, they must be miserable in it; for it is manifestly better,
not to be at all, than to subsist in misery.

And does, then, their perfect and
boasted religion of Nature bring them at
last to this unnatural pass, that they will,
upon the basest of motives, and contrary
to their own nature and to the intention,
of their all - beneficent God, who has
made them for an infinitely better existence than that of this life, and such glorious enjoyments in it, will they pin themselves down to the transitory, insignificant
gratifi-

gratifications of this prefent world, and wifh for nothing more, nay, that there might be no more, but all end with this life? Let there be but a place of any confiderable profit or honour offered to any of them, and how will he rejoice in it, and what difficulties will he not go through to obtain or preferve it? And how is it, then, that this man fhall fpurn away from him the infinitely more valuable offer of an endlefs poffeffion of inconceivable glory and happinefs? This perfon may, in this, certainly fee his own bafenefs, unreafonablenefs, and demerit: but, as we made not ourfelves, nor can alter that conftitution of things which the divine will hath eftablifhed, it is our chief bufinefs, in effect our only bufinefs, moft carefully and impartially to enquire whether thefe moft important matters be not fo as Chriftianity has re-

C. 4.   prefented

prefented them; and, if they be, to conform ourfelves to them; for other-wife we may, and defervedly fhall, undo ourfelves by this moft unreafonable and criminal neglect.

CHAP.

C H A P. III.

CHRISTIANITY tell us, that there is to be another life after this, and that it ſhall be a ſtate of retribution ; and the natures both of God and man tell us the ſame. The Heathen philoſophers, through their ignorance of the divine Being, and his moral and particular government of the world, could make nothing of this argument. Seneca, as well as Mr. Gibbon, tells us, that although they had promiſed, yet they had not proved, this future exiſtence : but it is not ſo with them whom Chriſtianity has enlightened.

Man is a moral creature ; and to be moral, is to deſerve love and reward,

or

or hatred and punishment, for his good or evil behaviour : he feels that it is so. The divine Being is likewise moral, moral in the highest possible degree ; and must, therefore, have these affections to the man, and see that he merits the one or the other of these retributions. And shall he not deal with him in a manner conformable to them ? This would be a direct contradiction to both their natures ; and, therefore, he must, as certainly as he is moral himself, and much more as he is the moral governor of the world, reward the one, and punish the other. And as this retribution is not always, perhaps never, adequately administered in this world, it must be so in another ; and that constitution of Nature, which the Creator of the world hath established, demonstrates that it shall be so.

All

All happiness depends upon virtue ; and, to be complete in happiness, we muſt be entire in virtue : for wherever vice is admitted, miſery muſt be there. If, then, the all-gracious God hath deſigned us for any happineſs hereafter, and much more for a happineſs which is to be complete and certain, he muſt breed us up to virtue here ; for we are made every-thing, we are even made reaſoners, by exerciſe and habit : and if we ſhall accuſtom ourſelves to contradict and deſpiſe the obligations of virtue for the love of ſenſuality and vice, we muſt, by a natural neceſſity, render ourſelves incapable of happineſs hereafter, and plunge ourſelves into miſery and ruin ; and remain in this miſery till we have changed our nature, and made that virtuous and good which was before vicious and bad. Religion and virtue are, then, the moſt important

portant of all matters ; and the infidel neglect of them the moſt irrational and deſtructive that can be. We muſt in this life take care to habituate ourſelves to love and to chuſe the things which are good, and to abominate and caſt from us the things which are evil. And man's own nature ſhews him that this was the very end of his creation, and the cauſe of his being introduced into the preſent world.

That man is deteſtable and vicious who is not governed by virtue ; and virtue always requires, that, in the things concerning itſelf, we act above this world; and, where any competition comes between the intereſts of the two, that we act in direct contradiction to the latter, and ſacrifice all the enjoyments of life, nay, and life itſelf, to the obligations of virtue ;

virtue ; and this too, although it should
be by the most painful of deaths.   And
so certainly as man's nature requires this
of him, so certainly does it prove that
he was made for a future life, and a just
retribution in it : for, otherwise, his moral
and all-gracious Creator and Governor
must have caused him to lose all enjoyment, nay, and his existence too, for
the doing of that which he wills and requires him to do, must love him for
having done, and for which he must see
that he deserves a reward ; and the
higher reward, the more he acts in this
manner.   These things cannot be, it is
impossible that they should be ; and
therefore a future life, and a just retribution in it, are as certain to those who
truly know their God, as that there is
such a Being, and that he made and go-
verns the world.   And, in fact, a notion
of

of this kind is fo natural to man, that it has generally prevailed over the whole earth; and we can hardly find any nation, however barbarous, in which this has not been their belief; but fo obfcured and perverted, where Chriftianity did not enlighten them, that it became ufelefs, and even ridiculous, to the thinking part of mankind.

How juft and beneficial, then, is Chriftianity, which hath opened and afcertained all thefe moft important matters to us, and affured us all of everlafting life, glory, happinefs, upon the eafy terms of the Gofpel? And what fhall we think of that perfon, who, by deftroying Chriftianity, would ftrip us of that hope fo glorious in itfelf, and always fo neceffary to cheer us in the many misfortunes of this prefent life, and which would, at the

same

same time, nearly reduce this world to a hell of wickedness and misery; for the taking away all expectation of a future life, or retribution in it, must produce all these horrible effects : it must give to our animal and brutish appetites and paf-fions, the entire dominion over the man, and thereby annihilate every thing which is worthy of esteem, or productive of happiness, and throw him into every vice which is most debasing and hurtful ; and this not only to others, but even to himself. And thus having opened and vindicated the truth and benefit of Chrif-tianity in the foregoing most important particulars, upon the mistaking of which the greater part of our modern infidelity is founded, I shall proceed to examine Mr. Gibbon's objections against this re-ligion, and return, as I hope, a satis-factory reply to them.

CHAP.

C H A P. IV.

IT is certain, from Mr. Gibbon's declaring the polytheiftick worfhip of the Heathens to be all foolifh and falfe, and yet avoiding to give any commendation to that of the Chriftians, which is all confined to the one true God, and is a fpiritual fervice befitting his fpiritual and infinite nature; but, on the contrary, blaming them for refufing all communication with the heathens, in their religious offices;—it is certain that he muft totally condemn all adoration of God as a piece of fuperftition and folly. But, as Chriftianity and Judaifm, upon which it is founded, have laid the greateft ftrefs upon this matter, and made divine worfhip the firft of all duties, it is become

abfolutely

abfolutely requifite that we enquire into the neceffity and reafonablenefs of this worfhip ; and this not only for the confutation of unbelievers, but alfo for the conviction of many of thofe who call themfelves Chriftians, but, by the fophifms of our infidels, have been drawn into fuch a neglect and contempt of this great duty, as a total rejection of Chriftianity, and indeed of all religion, can alone vindicate.

I will not fuppofe my antagonift to be an atheift, but a theift and a believer of God and his attributes ; and upon this foundation will I argue the cafe with him. It is the office of reafon to make us enquire and know, and principally in thofe things which are moft excellent in themfelves, and important to us. And as the being and nature of God, his govern-

D   ment

ment of the world, our dependence upon
and obligations to him, and the returns
which it is proper we should make for
them, are of all other subjects the most
noble and interesting, so must it be the
principal end for which reason was given
us, the chief of its offices, and our most
important business to enquire into, and
make ourselves knowing in, all these matters. And upon any proper enquiry, we
must find our God to be the Creator of
all things, that they all do subsist but by
his will, and every one of them depend
upon him for its being, and all the blef-
fings which any creature possesses. And
we shall likewise find that he is so perfectly excellent in himself, and so infinitely good to men, as to deserve all the
esteem, reverence, love, thankfulness,
which our hearts can contain : and when
a sensibility of these things has been acquired,

quired, we muſt ſee it to be our duty, and the firſt of all duties, to entertain ſuch affections for him, as are ſuitable to his all-perfect nature and our obligations, and from hence know, that we ought to take all proper means to entertain, preſerve, invigorate, and expreſs theſe ſentiments to him ; and as ſoon as the ſoul has contracted theſe diſpoſitions, we ſhall proſtrate ourſelves before him in the moſt humble adoration of dependence, love, truſt, gratitude, praiſe.

Neither is this grateful homage our duty only, but alſo our higheſt intereſt. Although man be at the head of our world, there is not any animal in it which has ſo many wants, and is of himſelf ſo little able to ſupply them. He is, indeed, that great beggar who ſubſiſts upon the joint alms of the whole creation.

D 2　　　　　There

There is no other animal who feels such
want of enjoyment, that is subject to
so many evils, and suffers so often and
grievously, as he; none of them which
are so insecure in their blessings, nor
troubled with those reasonable fears and
anxieties which so often fill and torture
the human breast: and if every man ex-
periences these wantings in the affairs of
this life, how much more does the re-
ligionist feel them in those of his eternal
concerns! This is unquestionably his
case; and by these wants, as well as his
own natural inclinations, is he urged on,
is he almost compelled to look out for
some superior being, upon whose goodness and power he may depend for protection and for succour, suitable to his
many dangers, and all his craving wants.
And to his greatest possible advantage,
he may have all this in his almighty and
most

moſt loving and kind God ; for he himſelf has aſſured him, that he will, upon
his properly aſking them in prayer, ſave
him from every evil, and bleſs him with
every good, ſo far as theſe ſhall be really
beneficial to him. What an ineſtimable
benefit, then, is this Chriſtian worſhip to
men ! when we, who muſt care for all
theſe things, know that we can thus lay
all our care upon one who careth for us,
and is always as willing and ready, as he
is powerful and mighty, to protect and
ſave us.

But this is not all : the divine Being
ſtands in another relation to man, which
is of all others the moſt important, and
to which he ought. moſt carefully to attend ; namely, that he is the moral governor and judge of the world ; which
relationſhip, beſides adding another rea-

D 3   ſon

fon for divine worſhip, will introduce a
new and different ſpecies of it.

We know that the heaven of heavens
cannot contain him, that he fills the
whole of creation, and all ſpace, which
is infinitely beyond it, and is more intimately preſent to every creature than any
creature can be to itſelf, and underſtands.
much better whatſoever it thinks or acts;
and with this abſolutely perfect knowledge of them all, we know that he muſt,
both from the nature of himſelf and his
government, reward or puniſh men for
their good or evil behaviour here. As
man is, then, a ſinner, and obnoxious to
the divine vengeance, ſo muſt he, in his
adoration, addreſs his God with thoſe ſentiments and expreſſions which are ſuitable
to his ſinful condition. He muſt, if he
will hope for the ſo exceedingly wanted
mercy.

mercy and pardon from his offended God, who cannot be deceived, and is of too pure eyes to behold, or bear with, iniquity,—he muſt conceive and declare his ſenſe of, and ſorrow for, his ſins, confeſs them all to him, humble himſelf for them, reſolve to amend them, and implore the forgiveneſs of them, and the divine aſſiſtance to enable him to conquer them hereafter, and live a more virtuous life. That ſinner, and every man is a ſinner, who does not thus humble himſelf before his God for his manifold tranſgreſſions, has no knowledge of himſelf or the great Governor of the world, nor any ſenſe of, nor repentance for, ſin ; and neither deſerves nor is capable of mercy or happineſs whilſt he continues ſuch : for, without a reformation of ſoul, he is diſqualified for both of theſe ; and he can have no reformation till he is filled

witl

with thofe difpofitions and fentiments
which I have now defcribed.

And here it is to be obferved, that, as
the great end of all true religion and religious worfhip, is to qualify men for the
favour and happinefs of God, and neither of thefe is poffible to be obtained
but by virtue, fo muft all true religion
tend to make us virtuous:—and as no
means can be fo powerful for this purpofe as thofe which fhall beget in us an
unfailing and moft lively fenfe of the being of a God, and his conftant infpection
of, and regard to, our behaviour, as our
juft governor and judge,—and prayer
is the beft means poffible to preferve and
enliven this fenfe, as alfo to breed in our
hearts all thofe affections which are moft
virtuous and inciting to virtue,—fo is it
from hence manifeft, that prayer is not
only

only the firſt but the moſt important of
all duties; for to love that incomprehen-
ſible Being who is all perfection, loveli-
neſs, goodneſs, and bliſs, with all our
heart, with all our ſoul, with all our
mind, and with all our ſtrength, is, both
from reaſon and revelation, the greateſt
of all the commandments; and prayer is
the breeding, exerciſing, and improving
all theſe affections in us.

It is from hence now equally plain and
certain, that it muſt prove a direct contradiction to the whole reaſon and nature
of religious worſhip, to offer it up to
any other than the one true God? And
could, then, the primitive Chriſtians join
with the Heathens in their religious ſervices? No! To have given this to the
higheſt and pureſt of angels would have
been idolatry; and how much more ſo
when

when these were performed to such a-
bominable creatures, and in such abominable rites as the Heathen worship con-
sisted of!

Besides, as the innocent and necessary
business, refreshments, and amusements
of this life must totally engross the man,
if there were not some proper means appointed by which to take off his attention from them, and fix it upon his infinitely more important concerns of futurity, so is prayer of all others the most
forcible to work this effect upon him..
And now let my reader think what an.
invaluable privilege it is to have the Almighty Governor of the world ever open
to our petitions, and ready to grant them ;.
and what a benefit Christianity has con-
ferred upon us in preserving and making
acceptable our proper worship ; and what.

an

an infinite prejudice it muſt do to the
world, to have both this religion and religious adoration totally deſtroyed! In
this have we a ſignal inſtance of the uncertainty and great imperfection of that
religion of nature, as it is called, which
our infidels would ſet up, and are uſed ſo
mightily to extol, when the great genius and learning of Mr. Gibbon could
not yet diſcover that religious worſhip
was at all a duty, or appropriated to the
one true God.; but he holds it all to be
a piece of ſuperſtition and folly. It is
not, however, a duty to be admitted by
any deiſt; for this conceſſion would neceſſarily imply, that the divine Being
had a regard to the behaviour of men,
and was governor of the world : and
this implication would ſo mightily diſ-
turb the quiet of thoſe gentlemen who
think, with Lord Bolingbroke, that they

can.

can have no reason to fear God, though
there should be a future life, for he can
never do any of his creatures any harm,
that this was by all means to be rejected
from their belief. And here, too, we
have a signal instance of what the gene-
rosity and boasted dignity of these gentlemen amount to; who, instead of being moved to virtue by this unbounded
goodness of their God, do, from hence,
take occasion not only to neglect him
and his particular duty, but to run into
the most shameful and pernicious wickedness that the fashion of the world, or
a regard to their own reputation, will
allow of.

And having now seen what Heathenism was, and Christianity is, and how
exceedingly absurd and abominable the
former, even in the most polished, in-
quisitive,

quifitive, and knowing nations ; and how
entirely true, ufeful, confiftent, and important the latter ; it will be eafy to obferve, that he muft have a mind deeply
prejudiced, who does not here difcern the
certainty and truth of the Chriftian religion, and that founded not only on reafon, but in its goodnefs and happy effects ; and fee that it muft come from
that infinitely beneficent Being, who loves
and would make happy all his creatures,
not willing that any fhould perifh, but
that all fhould come to everlafting life.

CHAP. V.

MR. Gibbon, in page 536, accounts for the prevalence of the Chriſtian reli-gion in theſe words: *It was owing to the convincing evidence of the doctrine it-ſelf, and the ruling providence of its great Author.* What pity it is that this gentle-man does not always write in the ſame manner!—but afterwards, with a mani-feſt inconſiſtency, applies all his endea-vours to extirpate this religion, which in this place he ſo juſtly commends for its uſefulneſs and truth. But leaving this to his own heart, whether for ridicule or ſe-riouſneſs, I am to obſerve, that one moſt material proof for our religion is here totally ſuppreſſed; namely, the very nu-merous and ſtupendous miracles which
Chriſt

Christ and his Apostles worked for the confirmation of their divine mission; and which, as Dr. Watson obferves, are in the Scriptures fo interwoven with their doctrines, that it is impossible to separate them the one from the other; and which, although they had all ceased with the lives of the Apostles, were yet fo authentically fet forth by them in a most undoubted history, that all men might be as certain of them as if they had been the objects of their own fenfes. Never men gave fuch proofs of their integrity as the writers of them did; and all that they delivered was from their own certain knowledge, for they had feen and heard them. Nor were thefe miracles wrought in a dark corner, or in the prefence of friends, to cover up or promote an impofture, or to prove things pleafing to the world, or where the great of it could be

be flattered by them ; but it was to introduce a new and abominated religion,
and in the prefence of adverfaries, the
moft eager and fpiteful againft them, and
in a moft knowing nation, who had all
power in their hands, and were, by the
ftrongeft ties both of intereft and inclination, driven on to difcover and ex-
pofe the cheat, if any thing of that kind
could be found in them ; but who, by
authentic proofs drawn from their own
writings, are fhewn to have acknowledged them : only by afcribing them to magick, they deftroyed their effects, and
even made them the fubjects of ridicule
to their own people. Let us, however,
go on to confider fome of the internal
evidences which our author himfelf allows to be in Chriftianity.

For a proper reprefentation of this matter,

ter, in many of the moſt ſtriking inſtances, I am happy in being able to refer the reader to Mr. Jenyns's late book
upon this ſubject, who was once as much
prejudiced, and wrote as perniciouſly, a-
gainſt Chriſt's religion, as Mr. Gibbon
himſelf; but to whom a thoughtful hour,
when the vanities of this world ceaſed to
have an undue influence upon his mind,
brought conviction along with it; and
this upon ſuch juſt and forcible reaſons,
that, if Mr. Gibbon will as juſtly confider them, as they are juſtly ſet forth, they
will make a believer of him as they did
of Mr. Jenyns. This being, however,
a moſt important ſubject, I will add ſomething both to its internal and external
proofs.

The latter gentleman, with the greateſt
truth, obſerves, that before Chriſtianity

E   there

there exifted nothing like true religion upon the face of the earth, except only among the Jews, who were enlightened by Chriftianity's precurfor; for all of the Heathens, as held by their greateft reafoners and wifeft philofophers, was falfehood, fuperftition, idolatry. But Chrift was a carpenter, and the reputed fon of a carpenter; and his Apoftles, all of them, illiterate, and the moft of them poor ignorant fifhermen: and yet thefe low people have given to the world fuch a compleat rule of duty both to God and man, that there is neither fuper-abundance nor deficiency in it; but where the fharp eyes of a Shaftfbury condemns, and would have it amended, he would have but perverted and fpoiled the whole by the propofed change. Thefe men, too, fet forth in their writings a fcheme of providence fo very high and wonderful, and fo well
adapted

adapted to, and explanative of, the ancient and previous revelation of the Jews,
that we may fafely pronounce the inven-
tion of it to be far beyond all human
wifdom, and much more the wifdom of
thefe ignorant, poor Apoftles.

Thefe illiterate men alfo give us the
hiftory of the life, actions, teaching, of
a man who affumed a character great beyond imagination, and to which nothing
in this world was equal, or had any likenefs to it; namely, of his being both
God and Man. And have they, indeed,
made him act up to this claim? Let the
reader know, to his aftonifhment, they
really have; that they have done it in
every inftance, and where the things were
moft ftupendous and difficult; where
they were to fill up this feemingly contradictory character, long before defcribed

in

in many prophecies, and to be manifest-
ed by a feries of miraculous works,
which were totally beyond all human
powers, and in which the greater part
of this character was directly repugnant
to their own expectations, their deepeft
prejudices, and all their hopes and comfort in this world ; and the whole of thefe
tranfactions defcribed in the moft plain
and artlefs narration that ever was pen-
ned : and all this with a difcovery of their
own great faults, their worldly-minded-
nefs, ftupidity, and perverfenefs ; and
their mafter's reprehenfions for them.
Here have we internal evidence indeed ;
and I will, befides, add to it an external
proof likewife.

It was impoffible that the Apoftles
could be deceived, or deceivers ; and
therefore their teftimony is true. They
muft

muſt have known whether Chriſt taught
ſuch doctrines, worked ſuch miracles,
died upon the croſs, was buried, roſe a-
gain from the dead, and proved himſelf
to be alive again by many infallible to-
kens ; they muſt have known whether
he did, according to the promiſe made
them whilſt he was alive, ſend down upon them, after his death, the gifts of his
Holy Spirit, whereby to make them
know and receive his true religion, a-
gainſt which they were before moſt in-
veterately prejudiced ; — to underſtand
and ſpeak a variety of languages, with
which they were before totally unac-
quainted ; to enable them, in conſequence
of his previous promiſe, to perform the
ſame miracles which he had done in confirmation of their divine miſſion, and to give
to theſe former worldlings and cowards ſuch
a contempt for this world, ſuch a regard

for

for the truth, the falvation of men, and
the rewards of virtue in a future life;
and fuch an undaunted daring fpirit in
doing the thing which was right, as
caufed them, though before well warned
of the fatal confequences of the thing,
to go about and preach Chrift's religion
to every nation under heaven; and to
perfevere in this work againft all the perfecutions which malice, power, cruelty,
could inflict upon them, even to the moft
torturous of deaths. Thefe things they
muft have all known; it was impoffible
for them to be deceived in any of them;
and yet their Mafter, in fending them out,
puts their miffion upon fuch a bottom,
as renders it impoffible for them to be
deceivers.

For as he did, contrary to all the ends
of impofture, fix the truth of his own
office

office upon his undergoing the moſt igno-
minious treatment, and cruel death; ſo did
he ſend out his Apoſtles upon the ſame
footing. His own words are, Behold I
ſend you forth as ſheep among wolves:—
ye ſhall be betrayed by fathers, mothers,
ſiſters, brethren; ye ſhall be called before
kings for my ſake, ſcourged in their ſynagogues, put to death, and ſo hated of
all men, that he who killeth you will
think he doth God ſervice. Very ſtrange
it is, that ſuch a religion as theirs ſhould
produce ſuch an effect; but he fore-ſaw
and predicted it to them: theſe predictions they every where publiſhed where-
ever they preached, and theſe miſeries
they were therefore as certainly to meet
with, as their preaching was true: and
they alſo told to their converts, that they
ſhould experience the ſame, and it proved ſo; and yet they not only undertook,

E 4 but

but perfevered in, this moft difficult, dangerous, and unpromifing work, and endured, in the profecution of it, fuch oppofition, hatred, inflictions, as it is hard
to think how human nature could rifque,
or any refolution enable them to bear
them. Let the reader turn to 2 Cor.
11 chap. where St. Paul is forced to give
an account of his own fufferings for the
preaching the Gofpel, and he will find
this thoroughly exemplified. And all this
done by them, not to obtain any worldly
advantage, but an excefs of mifery, and
for the fole purpofe of turning men away
from every vice to every kind of virtue,
and to the practice of every duty which
can adorn and perfect human nature, and
render men fit for the favour of their all-
holy God, and that everlafting and inconceivable happinefs which he hath
created them for:—a proceeding this,
which

which never could have flowed from any other fource than fuch an uprightnefs of foul as made them incapable of any deceit.

These are but a very few of our evidences for Chriftianity ; and had the ingenious and learned Mr. Gibbon given a proper attention to them, few as they are, we never had been hurt, nor his country neither, by the infidel part of his book.

CHAP.

CHAP. VI.

NUMBERLESS paffages in the Hiftory fhew that the author of it intended
it to deftroy Chriftianity entirely ; and yet
p. 535, it is with him a pure, humble, and
commended religion. This is very furprifing, but poffibly it may be accounted
for : poffibly he may fuppofe Chriftianity to be what Dr. Tindal would feem to
make of it, a republication of the religion of Nature ; which, although Chrift
and his Apoftles were a fet of deceivers
and profligate liars, yet have they given
to the world in a much more perfect
manner than any others ever did ; only
they have mixed with it a great many
falfehoods, and incredible facts ; and,
what is worft of all, have given men
occafion

occafion to fear, as well as to hope, by
the declarations of it.

Page 537, the religion and worfhip of
the Jews are manifeftly condemned, and
Herodotus's account of their circumcifion
preferred before that of the Scriptures,
which tell us, that Abraham received it
from God, and upon a particular occafion, and not from the Egyptians : but
to which of them we ought to give credit, to them or an author confeffedly fa-
bulous in many inftances, it is eafy to
fee. There is nothing elfe worthy notice
in that page ; only that the abufe of the
Jewifh religion is taken from Heathen malice and ignorance, and not from the
truth. Page 538, the miracles which he
would have afcribed to the convenience
of the Ifraelites, fhould have been fet
down for the good of mankind, for the
manifefting

manifefting the true God, and his true
religion and worfhip, which were then
moft miferably miftaken by the whole
world ; thofe only excepted whom he had
enlightened by his own law. The pretended incredulity of the Jews has been
fhewn by Dr. Watfon to be a miftake ;
Chriftians, without abandoning their faith,
are often tempted to diftruft, and mur-
mur againft, Providence. But, befides the
Ifraelites, thofe great miracles of Mofes,
&c. muft have been known to all the
nations around them, and have had a
very powerful effect to bring them back
to the true religion, and the knowledge
and worfhip of the one true God, from
which they were all then moft horribly
eftranged.

Page 539, the Jewifh eftablifhment
was juftly appointed by a good God, not
for

for conqueft, but for the people's fafety.
The end of all true religion is virtue, and
virtue is never promoted, but always deftroyed, by conquefts and large dominion ;
and, therefore, the Jews, although a very
numerous and powerful nation, were never able to obtain a territory of any confiderable extent ; and this was peculiarly
the cafe whilft they were under God's
more immediate government, by his
Judges. That they worfhipped the one
true God, and him only, and with a fervice fuitable to his fpiritual and infinite
nature, although here reprefented in an
indifferent light, was to them, in reality,
the higheft honour and the greateft advantage.   Page 541, Chriftianity is here
confeffed to be founded upon, and armed
with, the Jewifh law, and yet this law is
all along condemned by Mr. Gibbon ; and
from hence we can eafily difcern what he
thinks

thinks of this religion. The eternal life of glory, assured to every virtuous person by the Gospel, warranted the most ardent zeal for it; and Christ's command to his Apostles to go out and preach this religion to all the world, and throughout such difficulties and sufferings, proved that it came from the almighty and beneficent God, who can govern all creatures as he pleases, and make the meanest instruments effect the greatest purposes; who would do every thing possible to benefit his creatures, and would most amply reward his faithful servants for any thing they had suffered upon his account; that is, for doing good to his world.

Page 542, Mr. Gibbon's words are: *Every privilege that could raise the proselyte from earth to heaven, that could exalt his devotion, secure his happiness, or even gratify that secret pride which, under the*

the semblance of devotion, insinuates itself into the human heart, was still reserved for the members of the Christian church. Was it a fault in Christianity, that it prepared men, by a Christian and pure life here, for a heaven of perfect happiness hereafter ; and assured those who were so prepared, of obtaining this inconceivable blessing ? And is it a fit epithet for Christian devotion, because it brings us into an intercourse with the Divine Being, and makes us certain of being accepted by him, to call it a gratification of pride ? Or can, indeed, that religion render us proud, which tells us that our only worth arises from another, and that we are in ourselves incapable of any access to God, even in our very best services ? What can this gentleman's notion of religion be ? If we are at all to pray, must it not be in hopes of being favourably heard ;

and

and if we can be fure that we are fo, muft it not give us delight? Chriftianity has fhewn us that we are made for ever-lafting happinefs, and that the means to obtain this happinefs is virtue, and Chrif-tianity is abundantly proved; and, there-fore, as it muft be moft virtuous to re-ceive, fo muft it be criminal to reject, fuch a religion, and fuch a conviction as this.

The enfranchifement of the Chriftian church from the Jewifh ceremonial law, was to the Jews a matter of great difficul-ty, and therefore of fome length of time. And no wonder, when it had the riveted prejudices and the exceffive pride of the Ifraelites, in being the chofen and pecu-liar people of God, to contend with and mafter before it could be received. The arguments here offered againft Chrif-tianity

tianity, are acknowledged to have met with a confutation : but this in such a manner as, in my opinion, to make them require a particular reply.

The immutability of the God of the Jews is no argument for the immutability of their law. The divine conftitutions muft be changed as the mutability and exigencies of that inconftant creature man fhall require. The religion of the patriarchs, before Mofes, was a divine law, as much as that which Mofes himfelf gave ; and yet his law made great alterations in it. All that could be wanted was a fufficiency for falvation, and this fufficiency might be obtained by various inftitutions, and different degrees of light. The great point of all was, along with

F   this,

this, properly to fore - shew and pre-
pare men for the reception of a Redeemer to come; and it might have
been, it must have been, most preju-
dicial to have the whole of the design
at once opened; it must have prevented the completion of it. God's providence is his infinite power, justice,
wisdom, goodness, put into action;
and it is most wickedly presumptuous
for any man to find fault with it, when,
to have any proper understanding of
the matter, the whole of the case, with
all the reasons upon which he acts,
must be made known to us. But man
can never see any thing like this; a
most inconsiderable part only can possibly be discovered by him; probably
not one link of the chain in a thou-
sand: and it is a signal instance of the
divine

divine contrivance, that he has enabled us men, at all, to account for his workings, and vindicate them in so many instances as we really can.

The repeal of the ritual law was more manifest than the establishment of it. The miracles wrought by Christ and his Apostles, were as great, and out of all comparison more numerous, than those of Moses and all the Prophets put together; and the law itself, besides all its typical services which pointed to Christianity, and received the whole of their value from this future dispensation, did, in many places, expressly declare, that it was to give way to, and be superseded by, a new and better covenant. Great caution was, however, necessarily to be used in this

F 2 matter,

matter, left it should give occasion to the Jews to despise and cast off this law before its time, (to which they were for a great while strangely inclined,) which was, in time, to bring them to Christ, and the rest of mankind along with them :—the principal design, and the very end, of the law.

That Christ and his Apostles observed it, is no proof of its perpetuity. These were all Jews, and therefore, in conscience, obliged to keep it as long as it lasted ; and this was till our Saviour's dying, rising again, ascending into heaven, the immediate presence of the Father, and sending down from thence the gifts of his Holy Spirit upon men, had fulfilled and abrogated the whole ritual part of the law. Modern discoveries

in

in the Hebrew have made it plain, that the moſt material of its rites were appointed to ſhadow forth our redemption in Chriſt.

A full knowledge of Chriſtianity was not at once given to the Apoſtles; they were not, for ſome time, *able to bear it:* and if it had been given, they might, without incurring the charge of ambiguity, which is here laid upon them, have acted as they did. They might yield to men's weakneſſes in innocent matters, rather than, by inſiſting upon them, to cut off many well-meaning, but deceived men, from all hope of ſalvation. This was the known practice of St. Paul. He conformed to the Jewiſh prejudices in ſome leſſer matters, to take away their offence a-

F 3   gainſt

gainſt Chriſtianity; but when the neceſſity of theſe was inſiſted upon, he
refuſed to conform, and utterly condemned and rejected them all. This
was alſo the deciſion of the great coun-
cil of Jeruſalem, ſo ſoon after Chriſt
that ſome of the Apoſtles aſſiſted in it:
and as certainly as Chriſt ſent out his
Apoſtles to preach his religion, ſo certainly was the opinion of the Judaiſing
Chriſtians falſe, that it was ſtill neceſſary to be circumciſed, and to keep the
law. Chriſt Jeſus came into the world
to ſave the whole of it, and not one
family only, or his own family more
than any other: father, mother, ſiſters,
and brethren, were they who kept his
commandments.

CHAP.

C H A P. VII.

THE four next pages I think of no confequence, but the 547th is a laboured attempt, by the means of the antient Gnofticks, to deftroy the Jewifh law ; as, by the means of this law, Mr. G. had before endeavoured to deftroy Chriftianity. And as these arguments are not replied to by Dr. Watfon, but a reference made to others for the confutation of them, I fhall, to fave the reader's trouble, myfelf give a particular anfwer to them.

Polygamy was permitted, but not enjoined, by the Jewifh law ; and our Sa-

F 4   viour's

viour's argument that only one woman
was at firft made for one man, when the
world moft needed population, was an unqueftionable proof that God fo intended
it, and that it always ought to be fo. David and Solomon were men, and therefore finners; but the former of thefe an
excellent man, though ftill a finner.
Men are made for a future life; it is
the great end of their being: and
when the religion and practice of any
people become incurably wicked, and
deftructive of that end, it then becomes the Divine Goodnefs utterly to
deftroy them; that fo he may hinder
others from being by them corrupted to
their deftruction, and by this paft
vengeance deter them from following
their wicked example. And thefe reafons are over and over again declared by
Mofes

Mofes to be the caufes of the Canaanites extirpation. The great Governor
of the world is not found fault with
for fending plagues, famines, and the
moft deftructive wars among men, to
punifh them for their wickednefs; and
how much better muft it ferve to this
purpofe, to make, profeffedly, another
people the executioners of his vengeance, whom he hath warned againft
thofe abominable crimes, and caufed to
inflict this punifhment upon them?—A
moft neceffary caution this to the people of our countries, and efpecially to
the propagators of infidelity among us:
for whenever the rejection of Chriftianity, and a wickednefs without fear,
becomes prevalent among us, it will
then be the cafe with us, as it was with
the Canaanites, and at laft with the
Jews

Jews themfelves; we fhall be totally deftroyed.

The Gnofticks had the whole world againft them as to bloody facrifices, and were as certainly wrong in condemning them before Chriftianity, as Chriftianity itfelf is true, which yet they pretended to believe. Thefe facrifices clearly fhewed, that fome expiation, befides the finner's repentance, was neceffary to take away fin; and that fin was fo exceffively odious to the Divine Being, that it could not be expiated but by the greateft poffible punifhment to the oblation, even the death of it. And the Jewifh law, befides, by making this facrifice an expiation for fin, and fo to fave the life of the finner, did manifeft, that a vicarious punifhment

nifhment fhould be accepted for him ;
and thus pointed out and prepared the
world for the receiving that ftupendous
atonement, which was to be made, in
due time, for the fins of all mankind,
by the death of the Son of God ; and
thereby fitted men for the embracing
that religion, which was to be founded
upon it, when it fhould be preached to
the world, and which, without this
previous preparation, we may certainly
conclude, would never have been embraced by it. Thefe were certainly the
ends of bloody facrifices ; although, it
muft be confeffed, that all the Gentiles, and the generality of the Jews,
had, for, a long time before, loft all juft
notion of them.

It is true, that the Mofaic law was
built

built upon temporal promises, the promises of the land of Canaan, and prof-
perity in it; but these were under-
stood, by the virtuous, as intended
to shew forth an infinitely better life
in the world to come. And if these
retributions, abstracted from this latter
expectation, be insufficient to combat
with the outrageous appetites and paf-
fions of men, when administered by human weakness and ignorance, as they
confessedly are, yet must they have a
much more powerful effect, when they
are dispensed by the hands of him who
can neither be resisted or deceived; and
more especially, as he had by many,
the most severe punishments, manifest-
ed his great displeasure to sin and vengeance against it; and had, besides, in
his law, given so many hints of a future

ture life, and a juſt retribution in it.
By theſe means muſt the temporal ſanc-
tions of the law have had a very powerful effect upon the Jews ; certainly, a
much more powerful effect than that
ſyſtem which our infidels are all endeavouring to introduce, who neither allow
any future life, nor a moral governor of
the world, nor any regard in him to
the behaviour of any man :—an important matter this, well worthy of thoſe
gentlemen's moſt ſerious conſideration,
who yet blame the Jewiſh law for its
deficiency in this matter, when they
themſelves are endeavouring to reduce
the world to an infinitely worſe paſs.

It is alſo to be added, that the moſt
merciful Judge of the world will certainly treat theſe comparatively ignorant

men

men with a greater lenity, and upon eafier terms of acceptance, than the others to whom he has communicated a greater degree of knowledge, and more powerful motives of obedience. And fo the Gofpel tells us it fhall be. The times of this ignorance God winked at. If nothing, however, of better information had been given to the Jews, they would not have been left in a worfe condition than the reft of mankind, who were to be faved as well as they: but even we can, in our weaknefs, difcover fome probable reafons why a future life of juft retribution was not yet thoroughly opened and afcertained to mankind; namely, that, till Chrift had, by his death, made atonement for the fins of the world, and, by his refurrection and afcenfion into heaven, and the merits

rits

rits of his entire obedience on our account, had procured us an entrance into
this place of everlafting blifs; it might
carry with it too great an extenuation
of the evil of fin (the heinoufnefs of
which it is the great bufinefs of all true
religion to manifeft and aggravate) to
make the blood of a beaft expiate fin,
and procure pardon and falvation to the
finner, and this in the favour, manfion,
and happinefs of an all-holy and juft God.
Befides, to have declared that any poffible obedience of finful man fhould
entitle him to this perfect happinefs,
would be at once to deftroy that whole
fcheme of redemption which the divine
wifdom, holinefs, goodnefs, had planned
for the falvation of the world, and all
true religion confequent of Adam's
fall: and to have openly foretold, that
this

this should be brought to pass by the obedience and death of the Son of God, must certainly have prevented the completion of the design ; for, then, neither would the Jews have crucified Christ, nor the devils have tempted them to it.

It is not true, that eternal damnation came upon all men by the fall of Adam. The atonement made by Christ (he is the lamb slain from the foundation of the world) extends to all mankind, whether living before or after him ; and will certainly save all those who acted up to the best light they could have. If God at all speaks to men, it must be in a manner intelligible to them ; and, therefore, in giving an account of his creating the world, he must express himself as working, as finishing his work

in

in fix days, as ceafing from it, as reft-
ing, and being refrefhed on the feventh.
But both Scripture and reafon tell us,
that we are to remove all imperfection
from thefe words when applied to him ;
and it is well known, that Mofes's de-
fcription of this matter is fo juft and
noble, as to have gained him an univerfal admiration ; and it is alfo to be
obferved, that, at the very time he ufes
thefe expreffions of refling, being refrefhed, &c. he tells us, God only
fpeaks, and the thing is created and
done.. The formation of Eve out of
Adam's rib, was neceffary to make
them both, and all mankind, who were
to defcend from them, one flefh ; and
to manifeft to them and all others, how
man and wife ought to love and be
joined to each other.   And as the want

G   of

of this rib in Adam was a perpetual memorial of this tranſaction as long as Adam lived; ſo was the want of a navel in them both an undoubted conviction that they were the firſt man and woman, and that they and the world were created by God, and received at ſuch a time their exiſtence from him.

The placing this pair at firſt in a garden, wherein was made to grow every plant which was good for food, ſight, or ſmell, was a proper means to make them, at once, acquainted with every production of nature, and thereby render them more ſenſible of, and thankful for, the divine goodneſs: as was likewiſe the bringing all the animals before Adam, that he might view and name them; who, by being able

to

to do this with such justice, that their
Creator himself approved of his names,
clearly manifests the wonderful perfection of man before his fall, and the ex-
cessive degradation to which this fall
has reduced him. The prohibiting
them only the fruit of one tree, out of
the prodigious profusion which abounds
throughout all the world, namely, of
the tree of the knowledge of good and
evil, was a positive command, and such
only could be given them in their state
of innocence and virtue : but this was
entirely proper to keep them ever mind-
ful of their God, and his government
over them, and their absolute dependence upon him ; as also, we may be
sure, to give them, in that state, the probation which was most necessary and
proper for the breeding them up to vir-

G 2   tue,

tue, and thereby fecuring to them, at
the laft, that perfect happinefs which
their good God intended and created
them for. And here it may not be
amifs to mention another inftance of
the Creator's care to imprefs a deep
fenfe of his dependence upon Adam's
mind. Eve was not formed till after
he had viewed every animal, and feen
them in pairs, and in company; and
how muft he have been affected to
have found himfelf, who the moft of all
wanted, and was the beft fitted for, fociety, totally deftitute of it? The whole
world muft then have appeared a defert
to him, and have made him defire, long
for, and eagerly pray to his God to
give him this fo much wanted compa-
nion; and this with fuch a pining after
it, as might well throw him into that
flumber

flumber or trance, wherein the rib was
taken out of him, Eve formed, and all
the rights of marriage revealed to him.
And when, by this inftance, as well as
many others, he was made duly fenfible
of his dependence upon God, behold
his wife is prefented to his view, all-
perfect, out of the hands of their gra-
cious God, and, to be fure, more lovely and beautiful, both in body and foul,
than any of that moft beautiful fex
has fince been.   Here had he an equal
caufe given him both for humility and
thankfulnefs.   The Devil, who was a
liar and a murderer from the beginning,
fpoke in the body of the ferpent, but
pretended that he both reafoned and
talked by the virtue of this forbidden
fruit, which he eat before the woman,
and thereby enfnared her and Adam ;

and

and it would have been to their everlafting ruin, had not the mercy of God
interpofed to fave them. Numberlefs
poffeffions of this kind, and even of
men, to fhew how man at firft fell, are
recorded in the Gofpel, by whofe or-
gans the devils fpoke and converfed.

The fall of Adam, which compre-
hended in it the fall of all mankind, is,
indeed, a very difficult fubject to fpeak
of; but in a matter of fuch exceeding
height and difficulty, it ought not to
be any argument againft it, that we
could not at all account for this providence, becaufe it is one of the moft
ftupendous,—in truth, it is in itfelf
the moft ftupendous of all the work-
ings of the one infinite Being who is
higher than the heavens above us; and
muft

muft infinitely tranfcend the reach of the wifeft of his creatures, till he himfelf fhall be pleafed more fully to open and declare the matter. But fome-thing he hath opened to us, and, with a proper confideration of that, we may poffibly come to fome knowledge of this providence.

The end of all God's creating and working is, moft affuredly, to commu-nicate happinefs. This end muft princi-pally be obtained by his making him-felf more known, who is perfect excel-lence, and muft ever be glorified by all his works, and fill all the higheft fa-culties of his higheft creatures with the greateft delight; and thofe works fhall beft anfwer this purpofe, which are made with fuch a variety as fhall, in

their

their formation, fhew more of his power, wifdom, goodnefs; and truly wonderful is that variety of every kind, which we experience in this our little world: and, as in our world, fo, certainly, in others, as well as in ours; and the different colours and fizes of the feveral planets in our fyftem make it plain that he has done fo in them. We are, then, to look for a wonderful peculiarity in his feveral worlds; and as in the worlds, fo in the creatures; and as in the creatures, fo in the providences by which they fhall be governed and conducted to their happinefs. It was the eternal purpofe of God to redeem man by Jefus Chrift: man's fall was therefore forefeen, and permitted to be brought about by the malice of the Devil; and, certainly, becaufe the divine wifdom and good-

goodnefs had determined to provide a remedy for the mifchiefs of it, which fhould at once do the moft honour to himfelf, and benefit to all his creatures, becaufe it fhould open his nature and beneficence in the moft aftonifhing inftances, and make this beneficence be productive of the greateft good.

Reafon and revelation equally fhew, that to be happy we muft be virtuous; and to be complete in happinefs, we muft be entire in virtue : and experience along with thefe equally manifefts, that we cannot have this unfailing virtue, but through the exercife and habit of a previous probation. The moft ftrengthening of all probations muft undoubtedly be the experiencing the mifery of fin, without being undone by the evil

of

of it : and, therefore, has the infinite wifdom of the Divine Being, and his goodnefs to his creatures, contrived a way to give man this moft neceffary and ufeful probation ; and this by the moft aftonifhing providence that his infinity has ever afforded, or ever will afford.

As all men were permitted to fall by the weaknefs and fault of one man, fo was it fitting, and, indeed, abfolutely neceffary, that they fhould be redeemed by the ftrength and virtue of another : and therefore were mankind fuffered to come into fuch a condition by the fin of Adam, as did neceffarily require that the goodnefs, nay, the juftice of the Creator fhould interpofe, and remedy this evil by fome extraordinary providence.

dence. And we find, by Chriftianity, that he has done fo; and has, at the fame time, moft benefited his creatures, and done the higheft honour to himfelf: for he has thereby given them the moft advantageous probation, and fhewn himfelf in the moft lovely and glorious light. I am confident that thefe reafonings are well founded and juft; and, if they be, what a monfter is our Deifm for its prefumption, ingratitude, folly!

To the charge of the God of the Jews being liable to paffion and error, capricious in his favour, implacable in his refentments, meanly jealous of his own fuperftitious worfhip, and confining his partial providence to a fingle people, and this tranfitory life, I need only,

only, after what has been already said,
obſerve, that, whenever his moral creatures change in their behaviour to him,
their great Governor muſt, in his affections to them ; that his abhorrence of
vice is the greateſt that can be, becauſe
moſt contrary to his own nature, and
deſtructive of all happineſs ; and that
the welfare of the whole world requires
him to manifeſt the moſt dreadful deteſtation of it ; that he is jealous of his
own worſhip, becauſe it is the firſt and
moſt important of all duties ; and that
it is a moſt palpable and ſtrange miſtake, to make him confine his providence to the Jews, when the Scriptures,
by ſo many and ſevere inſtances, ſhew
that he extended it alſo to the Gentiles.
And as to the laſt charge, that of his
chuſing the Jews for his own people,
and

and leaving the Heathens to themselves,
I reply, that, when we have a history of
God's moral government of the world
so well authenticated as that of the Old
Testament, it must be most presumptuous and criminal in any man, to find
fault with this dispensation upon his
own foolish conjecture. The one all-
wise Being may have many and the best
reasons for acting in such a manner, although every one of them should be
undiscoverable by us, and they should,
in our weak eyes, all of them seem contrary to wisdom and goodness, and even
to justice itself. But this is not the
case here; we can discern many reasons
for his leaving the Heathens to themselves, and taking the Jews into his peculiar protection and government, and
revealing himself and their duty to
them.

The

The former of these providences might be neceſſary to ſhew the ſad and ruinous condition of man when left to himſelf; and to manifeſt the abſolute neceſſity both of a Redeemer and of a Revelation, whereby not only to atone for ſin, but to inſtruct in righteouſneſs, and the virtuous means neceſſary to our future ſalvation : which neceſſity Mr. Gibbon knows to be even now denied by many people. And then, by God's winking at, and making proper allowances for, their almoſt invincible ignorance, this ignorance might be as. profitable, or more ſo, to their ſalvation, than a greater degree of light and knowledge. But, as the leaving the whole earth in ſuch exceſſive darkneſs might cauſe them to degenerate ſo far as would be deſtructive of all virtue and happineſs, and as the

chuſing

chufing one people to himfelf, and in-
ftructing them in his true religion and
virtue, and making it known that he
did himfelf govern all things, and would
not only reward the virtuous, but alfo
punifh the wicked, as by thefe means
he fhould do the more good to them,
keep the others to more knowledge and
better obedience, and give himfelf an
opportunity of reclaiming the reft whenever he fhould think fit; and as this
would require-fuch providences, not o-
therwife to be introduced, as would be
peculiarly honourable to himfelf, and
beneficial to his creatures; and, more
efpecially, as this particular law fhould
forefhew and keep up the expectation
of that wonderful Redeemer, who was
not immediately, but in the fullnefs of
time, to come into and fave the world;
fo,

fo, for thefe reafons, and, to be fure, infinite others unknown to us, was it
equally wife and good in the Creator
and Governor of all things to leave the
Heathens thus far to themfelves, and
take to himfelf the Jews for his peculiar people. And here we can certainly
fee, that the very ftubbornnefs and re-
bellions of this nation were of peculiar
fervice to the world ; as, by God's fo feverely punifhing them for their wickednefs, he demonftrated the falfehood of
that antient deftructive opinion of all
the philofophers, and this modern one
of all our unbelievers, that the God of
the world cannot hurt or make mifera-
ble any of his creatures. But I might
have cut fhort this defence ; for, let
the deifts fay what they will, they muft
either acknowledge polytheifm to be a
true

true religion, or confefs that God did
reveal himfelf to the Jews, and to the
Jews only.

And now the reader may fee that we
can effectually defend the holy fcrip-
tures of the Old Teftament againft
thefe felf-fufficient hereticks, without
having recourfe to any allegory, whofe
particular tenets were fo unreafonable
and ill-founded, that, were I to repeat
them, they would appear rather to de-
ferve the name of madmen, than that
of *knowers*, which they moft arrogant-
ly affumed to themfelves. And if the
primitive Chriftians did give a little into allegory, this is certainly to be ex-
cufed by Mr. Gibbon, who knows that
the philofophers were compelled to al-
legorize the whole of the Heathen re-
H   ligion

ligion, in order to make any defence at
all for it, and this with such a force and
absurdity, that it made them a ridicule
to some of their own people.

What credit their assertion of the
church's corrupting the Scriptures deserves, is manifest from hence, that
Christianity is as certainly founded upon Judaism, as Christianity is true ; and
yet all these Gnosticks condemned and
rejected that religion.   Tertullian tells
us, that the hereticks of his time were
wont to make the same false charge
against the church ; but he confutes
them, by appealing to all the great
churches founded and taught by the A-
postles, which, by all agreeing in one
doctrine, and this doctrine conformable
to that of the Scriptures, demonstrated
that

that this was the true faith, and not
that which those people set up in opposition to it. And it is manifest, that
the many diſſentions which were among
the Chriſtians themſelves, and which
made them a continual watch upon
each other ; the numberleſs copies taken, and every where ſpread abroad, of
the Scriptures ; and the many tranſla-
tions made of, and quotations taken
from them, muſt have rendered all wil-
ful and material corruption of them
utterly impoſſible.

Mr. Gibbon thinks, that, although
theſe people diſturbed the peace of the
church, they did not retard, but furthered,
the progreſs of it : but our Saviour was
of a different opinion, and ſo was another perſon too, not at all deficient in
H 2   cunning.

cunning. Chrift tells us, it was the Devil who fowed tares among his good feed of the word : and did he this, indeed, to ferve Chriftianity ? Does not Mr. Gibbon know, that the people of his principles, as well as the Papifts, make the uncertainty of the Scriptures fenfe, and the Chriftian diffentions about it, an argument againft our religion ? Can it be denied, that the Papifts did, by thefe means, put a ftop to the reformation, which otherwife threatened to annihilate the Romifh church ; and that they have ever fince been endeavouring to deftroy ours by the fame means, and did, for a time, accomplifh its ruin, in the reign of Charles I ? And is it any adequate advantage, that a diffenter is now and then gained over to this church, as was the cafe with Auguftine?

CHAP.

C H A P. VIII.

PAGE 552. We have here a keen ridicule upon the primitive Christians, for their notion of evil spirits, and their supposing them to be the authors of idolatry ; but, if they believed the Scriptures, they must have believed this : for what thinks he of these passages, and numberless others which might be produced ? " He was a liar and a murderer from the beginning ; the Devil entered into Judas ; the Gentiles sacrificed to devils, and not unto God ; all these will I give thee, if thou wilt fall down and worship me"—and of the numberless possessions recorded in the New Testament ? It may seem

strange

ſtrange and unaccountable to us, as it
did to Lord Bolingbroke, that ſuch evil
beings ſhould be ſuffered in the world
by a good God; but this only ſhews
us how little able we are to judge of
the divine ways. Nothing but the malice of theſe impure ſpirits could have
inſpired the impure, cruel, and murder-
ous idolatry practiſed by the Heathens:
and we find many of that caſt ſtill
among men—many powerful tyrants,
who deſolate whole nations by all the
rapines and cruelty of bloody and unjuſt wars; and many who are more
pernicious than they—many who employ the whole of their great abilities
to deſtroy all religion, and conſequent-
ly all happineſs either here or hereafter,
and reduce, even this world, to a hell
of miſery. But this diſbelief of devils

is

is a neceſſary part of the deiſtical nega-
tive creed : for, if angels, ſo much ſu-
perior to men, could yet, by their
wickedneſs, be ſo loſt to all virtue and
happineſs, it might be, it muſt be ſo
with men likewiſe ; and then there
would be room for thoſe fears in the
hearts of profligates, which it is the
great end of our infidelity totally to ex-
pel. And here it is to be obſerved,
that our modern deiſts all go againſt
their own ſcriptures ; namely, the opi-
nions of the philoſophers in this matter ; for they, with the Chriſtians, all
acknowledged the reality of theſe evil
beings, which our modern infidels do
all deny and ridicule.

As to the great caution of the Chriſtians, not to join in any of the Heathen

idolatries,

idolatries, they had abundant reasons for it. " Thou shalt worship the Lord thy God, and him only shalt thou serve," was to them the first and greatest of all commandments, and therefore ought to be the most strictly observed. But here I cannot help expressing my astonishment at Mr. Gibbon's making the want of intercourse between them and the Heathens, which this must necessarily occasion, the first of his causes for the growth of Christianity, when it was so manifestly fitted to obstruct the same. That it contributed to its preservation, cannot, I think, be denied ; for had the Christians joined themselves to the Heathen worship, it must, in my opinion, have hurt or annihilated their religion : but, although this was a necessary means of preserving Chris-

tianity,

tianity, it cannot be fet down for the furthering its growth, but by fuch a far-fetched and indirect inference, that, I am confident, Mr. Gibbon will not infift upon it.

The fecond of his fecondary caufes is, the doctrine of the foul's immortality. He feems, a few pages before, to believe this future immortality, and a juft retribution in it; yet, here he attributes the reception of them in the eaftern countries to an eftablifhed prieft-hood, which employed the motives of virtue as an inftrument of ambition. But certainly he might have difcovered a better reafon for this moft important belief: he might have founded it upon a notion fo natural to man, that it has generally prevailed over the whole world,

and

and even in the moſt barbarous nations; and upon an intercourſe in the Eaſt with the patriarchs and Jews, who all expected this future exiſtence, who had many hints for it in the writings of Moſes, and open declarations of it in the Pſalms and the Prophets; and in the book of Job (at leaſt as ancient as any of the Scriptures) a probable reaſon was given why it was not entruſted to the hereditary prieſthood of Aaron. But this is only an objection againſt Providence, which ought never to be made; becauſe we can never judge of this matter with any propriety, till we can, and do, ſee all the reaſons upon which the Divine Being acted; which is utterly impoſſible to men, or, indeed, to any creature.

Page

Page 560, he afferts, that all the
Jews, from Mofes to their return from
the captivity of Babylon, did not believe the foul's immortality, although
he had before acknowledged that many
expreffions in the Prophets did indicate
fuch. And here I will return an anfwer to that objection againft the Jewish
law, that it was founded upon temporal promifes, and gave no notion of a
future life; which, that I might take
in the whole of the matter at one view,
I did referve to this place.

It is true that Mofes did found his
law upon temporal promifes; but thefe
were intended to reach beyond this
prefent world; and he has therefore,
in his writings, given us many hints
which are decifive for a future life:
that

that Adam was not to die if he did not tranfgrefs ; when he did tranfgrefs, and muſt experience a temporal death; that yet his ſeed was totally to conquer his enemy, which would neither have been done, nor prove a comfort to him, unleſs death was to be conquered like-wiſe ; that he was certainly to die for his fin, and yet an atonement made by ſacrifice for it, and accepted by God ; and that he called his wife's name Eve, in Hebrew Life, becauſe ſhe was to be the mother of all living, ra-ther of all life, or of him who was life ; that righteous Abel was killed be-cauſe he was righteous, and his ſacrifice accepted by God ; that Enoch was ta-ken away becauſe he walked with God and pleaſed God, who alſo left a pro-phecy, preſerved to the Apoſtles times, of

of God's coming in another life to
judge the wicked ; that God ftyled himfelf the God of Abraham, Ifaac, and
Jacob, fome hundred years after the
death of them, which phrafe fhewed
them to be itill in being, and him the
greateft good to them ; and this, too, by
the name of Elahim, which is, covenan-
ters by an oath or curfe, and this oath
certainly to redeem man. Thefe things
did abundantly prove a future exiftence,
and that of retribution, from the writings of Mofes alone. And, befides the
many declarations for this future hope,
in the Pfalms and Prophets, we have
Elijah and Elifha raifing the dead, and
the former of thefe vifibly afcending into heaven, to confirm this hope. And
we know, likewife, from the Epiftle to
the Hebrews, that it was the very intention

tention of the Jewish tabernacle and temple, and the most solemn service of them, to shadow forth our entrance into a heaven of the highest happiness, by the atonement which our Great High Priest and Redeemer was to make of himself for the sins of the whole world.

We may expect, then, to find the belief of the Jews directly contrary to Mr. Gibbon's assertion; and so it is undeniably proved to every Christian, by St. Paul, Heb. xi. 13. "And confessed that they were strangers and pilgrims upon earth." 14. "For they that say such things, confess plainly that they seek another country." 16. "A better country, that is, an heavenly." 32. "For the time would fail me to tell

tell of Gideon and Barach, and Sampson and Jeptha, David, Samuel, and the Prophets." 39. " And thefe all having obtained a good report by faith, received not the promife."

Page 561. He has my thanks for faying that the doctrine of life and immortality is dictated by nature, approved by reafon, and confirmed by the example and authority of Chrift ; for if any truth be in any of thefe matters, and more efpecially in the latter of them, Chriftianity is truth : and whether it were or not, if fuch a future life be received, it is manifeft, that wickednefs muft difqualify for the happinefs of it ; and then there muft be in every way an end of infidelity : for the certain knowledge which Chriftianity gives us

of

of this future life, and our falvation in
it, will take away all prejudice againft
this pure religion; and then it fhall be
us univerfally, as it will be reafonably,
embraced.

That the expectation of Chrift's immediate coming to judgment was not
juftly founded upon Scripture, has been
made certain by Dr. Watfon; I will,
however, add, for the farther clearing
of this matter, that every one acquainted with the expofition of the prophecies, knows that there is a figurative,
as well as a literal, meaning intended in
them.   Sir Ifaac Newton has a particular treatife upon this head, fhewing
that fun, moon, ftars, heavens, earth,
feas, &c. fignify kings, rulers, nations, peoples, civil policies; and that in
this

this fenfe, our Saviour's prophecy of the
deftruction of Jerufalem, was all fulfilled in that generation ; although, in the
literal fenfe, it fhall not be till the end of
this world.   St. Paul has convinced us,
as well as 17 centuries, that it was not
to be in his time.   2 Theff. ii. 2.

Page 562. The doctrine of the millennium is fo thoroughly cleared by Dr.
Watfon, that I fhall fay no more to it,
than that it is very ftrange in Mr. Cib-
bon to make the joys of a future earthly habitation have greater force to
promote Chriftianity than the joys of
God's own habitation, and an heaven
of unutterable blifs ; and this too, when
none but martyrs were to partake of
them.   It is alfo furprifing to make the
Chriftians threatening damnation to the

Heathens a principal motive of their
conversion, when these could hardly
have any intercourse with the others;
when they and their religion were so
hated and despised by them; when all
retribution was denied by all their philosophers; and when it was by this conversion absolutely required that they
should abandon every vice, and live the
most careful and virtuous lives in every
instance afterwards; and this too under
a more severe and certain ruin for their
being Christians, if they did not; and
when, too, we experience that these are
the very things, these threatenings and
these severe lives, which make so many
Heathens among us Christians at this day.
The double sense of the prophecies ex-
plains all those expressions of the precious stones with which the new Jerusalem

lem was to be built, upon which this gentleman plays with so great an *impartiality.*

As to the conflagration of Rome, and the world, and his attributing our sense of the former to our prejudices against Popery, I must say, that either he has not read the late Protestant writers upon this subject, or else he has a most unjust partiality to that corrupted, idolatrous, and bloody church. But this is not the only instance in which I have found the Deists favourable to Popery.

Page 567. His 3d cause of Christianity's growth, is the miraculous powers of the primitive Christians.

He says, with a sneer, the Deity suspended

I 2   pended

pended the laws of Nature for the benefit of religion. Be it so, then ; but
it was because religion is the happiness
of those creatures for whose benefit these
laws were inftituted. He quotes Irenæus for faying, the knowledge of fo-
reign languages, although communicated to others, was not so to him when
he preached the Gofpel to the natives of
Spain : but he ought to have known,
that this is an impofition put upon the
reader and him by Dr. Middleton ; for
Irenæus fays no fuch thing. Theophilus was right in not undertaking to raife
a dead man for the conviction of a noble Greek. It was the Divine Being
who was to work the miracle, and he
might find caufe to refufe it, although
to men it might feem ever fo proper.
The Apoftles themfelves could only
work-

work miracles when the all-knowing
Spirit of God urged them to it. Chrift
Jefus would not gratify Herod with the
fight of one miracle, although it might
have faved his life. His account of the
Chriftian infpiration is fo certainly falfe,
that the only thing to be faid in his vin-
dication is, that he never examined the
matter, but trufted to Dr. Middleton,
without reading the anfwers given to his
book ; which, to fpeak the truth of it,
is written with a prejudice and difingenuity the moft difgraceful to any caufe,
or to any author. Let any one but
read over 1 Cor. xiv. chap. and he will
fee that the Chriftian infpiration was
the fartheft in the world from being
an unreafonable furor or madnefs ; for,
ver. 32, " the fpirits of the prophets
were fubject to the prophets."

I 3   If

If this Doctor were treated in the fame way that he has treated the primitive Fathers, whom he fo feverely condemns for fome erroneous reafonings, and, as he will have it, mifreprefentation of facts, that they are not to be credited in any thing about religion, his own character would fuffer a great deal more than theirs has done by this kind of treatment. This gentleman makes ufe of great artifice and difingenuity to difcredit the miracles of the primitive Chriftians, and has inferted fome paffages in his book which equally difcredit all miracles in general; which paffages, though often called upon, he would never retract. This gentleman did, alfo, publifh a book againft prophecy, by which he would have rendered that proof of our religion equally nugatory

gatory and ridiculous, and thereby deftroyed the two great foundations of
Chriftianity ; and yet this author held
to his death an ecclefiaftical preferment
in our Chriftian church, and was very
angry, to the laft, that he could not
get in it a more ample provifion : and
ought we to give him any credit in thefe
matters ?

Tertullian's Apology was written to
the Roman magiftrates, upon their perfecution of the Chriftians ; and it is
hard to think that he would put the defence of his caufe upon a certain impofture. His words are, *I come now to*
things, and give you a demonftration,
from facts, that your gods and the dæ-
mons are the fame. Let a dæmoniac
be brought into court, and the fpirit

I 4   *which*

which possesses him be demanded by any Christian to declare what he is, and he shall as truly confess himself to be a devil, as he did before falsely pretend to be a god. If all these do not declare themselves in court to be devils, not daring to lie in the presence of a Christian, that Christian is willing to be taken for a cheat, and to answer for it in his own blood. It is to be observed, that all this was to be done in a Heathen court, and upon a person produced by themselves, and therefore certainly known by them, and liable to the most careful inspection, and where, too, all power was in their hands ; and there could therefore be no possibility of a Christian juggle. And now let any one judge whether that person could be right in his senses who would place his religion,

comfort,

comfort, life, and the lives of all his
proffeffions, upon fuch a defence, if
this defence were really falfe and an impofture. But left this proof fhould be
thrown off by a reference to Dr. Middleton's Free Enquiry, I fhall, for this
once, fubjoin an examination of his reafoning upon this head.

To fay that the Chriftians were then
too poor to have a fufficient number of
their Apologies tranfcribed, when fo very
few of them would have ferved this
purpofe; when they were fo numerous
in Bithynia long before this, as almoft
to annihilate the Heathen worfhip, by
Pliny's confeffion; when Tertullian
himfelf afferts, the fenate, the army,
&c. to be all full of them; and Cyprian did, not long after this, and in
this

this very place, raise above 800 pounds
at once, for the redemption of Christian
captives ; and Mr. Gibbon owns, they
did then make up a tenth part of the
city of Carthage :—to say that the Heathen magistrates did not think it worth
their while to enquire into these matters, when Pliny did put two women
to the rack for this purpose, and these
magistrates were every day examining,
imprisoning, torturing, banishing, con-
fiscating the goods of Christians, and
putting them to the most cruel deaths,
for their faith—to say that the Christians
had then a particular order of men to
take care of, and instruct and cure these
possessed people, providing lodgings in
their churches for them, when they
were just now so poor as not to get a
few books transcribed for the saving
thier

their lives and fortunes; when he has not any authority for such a supposition at that time, but many against it, as may be seen in Mr. Bingham's Christian antiquities; and we may be sure the Heathen magistrates would never suffer any of those to be brought into examination, nor could the Christians be able to collect and support them all—to say such things in confutation of Tertullian's challenge, and of almost all the other Christian writers before and after him—and Dr. Middleton says them all—speaks not any fairness of mind, but the deepest and most rancorous prejudice. And here I will advise Mr. Gibbon not to follow Mr. Voltaire, as he here has the Doctor, in his future history, when he comes to the worship of images in the Christian church; be-

cause

cause this great genius's account of this
matter is totally copied from Baronius,
and where the interest of the Roman
church is concerned, there cannot be a
more partial and unjuft hiftorian than
this very great and learned cardinal.

Page 570. It will readily be acknowledged, that the pretended miracles of
the church of Rome have much hurt
our religion with many people ; but it
ought not to be fo. Real miracles will
probably introduce a pretence to feign-
ed ones. And if it is confidered that
the Popifh miracles are only propagated
and believed where their religion entirely prevails, and no examination can be
made of them, it muft appear that this
is no juft argument againft thofe of the
primitive Chriftians, where every thing
was

was the reverfe with them; and yet they boldly required an examination of them by their moft powerful, obftinate, and cruel enemies:—a diftinction this fo manifeft, that it is wonderful how Mr Gibbon could overlook it, and fo confound times together, as to make it impoffible to fay when miracles did ceafe, becaufe always reported to continue in the church, when, both from this and the fettlement of Chriftianity, we can fee, how they gradually became unneceffary, and the certain falfehood of thefe contemptible late reports.

We find, from the replies given to Dr. Middleton, that feveral Chriftian writers of the 3d and 4th centuries did acknowledge miracles to be then very rare among them, and nearly to have
ceafed

ceased from the church; and we can easily discern the fitness of this proceeding. As Christianity was the power of God to salvation, it was absolutely necessary for him, if he intended us this salvation, to support it by his own miraculous power so long as this extraordinary interposition was requisite: and, considering the nature of his religion, that it had nothing in the world to recommend it, but all the pleasures, interests, prejudices of it, to obstruct and destroy its progress — and considering that these miraculous powers were scarcely less necessary after, than before, the death of the Apostles, and that many others, besides the Apostles, were, in their own times, endowed with these gifts—these things considered, we have the justest reason to believe they still

.continued

continued in the church, and that the teſtimony given of them by ſo many writers is well founded and true. But ſo ſoon as Chriſtianity was able to ſtand upon its own legs, ſo ſoon as men's prejudices againſt it were pretty well worn off, and the powers of this world were no longer its enemies, but became its friends and ſupporters, and it could, by the common courſe of nature, maintain and increaſe itſelf, then was it fit that this extraordinary interpoſition ſhould be gradually leſſened, and, at laſt, totally taken away. This reaſoning is manifeſtly juſt, and I can confirm it by an inſtance, which, I am confident, Mr. Gibbon will not controvert.

In the middle of the fourth century, when Julian, the apoſtate Emperor, in order

order to invalidate our Saviour's prophecy about the deſtruction of Jeruſalem and the temple, did call home the Jews to their own country, and employ both the power of this zealous people, and all the ſtrength of his own mighty dominions, to execute this purpoſe ; and when there were no human means, which could poſſibly defeat it, the hand of God did itſelf viſibly interpoſe, and, by ſhakings of the earth, which threw up the foundations, and fire burſting out, which conſumed the workmen and their work, compel them to deſiſt from and abandon the undertaking : and this miraculous fact is acknowledged in the hiſtory of Ammianus Marcellinus, who, as a Heathen writer, may be believed, and who, as writing againſt his own principles, muſt

be

be believed, in his account of this matter. And thus are the fuppofitions of
Dr. Middleton, and of Mr. Gibbon,
both of them deftroyed by a Heathen
atteftation, and mine as undoubtedly
confirmed.

Page 572. Fourth Caufe of the
growth of Chriftianity, the good lives
of the Chriftians.

It is certain, that all the primitive
apologifts did boaft of the virtue of the
Chriftians, and it is here acknowledged
to be a fact :—the purity of their practice was conformable to the purity of
their faith, and this in a world of a totally different caft :—which virtue effectually proved the truth of their religion, by the beneficial effects which
K flowed

flowed from the profession of it. And
no wonder, when no other religion in
the world ever taught such pure morality, and enforced it by the like powerful motives of an infinitely holy and
just God observing every action, and
rewarding or punishing it with an eternity of the greatest happiness or misery,
as the moral creature's behaviour should
deserve. In this had they such motives
as were fitted to produce this virtuous
life, and, in justice to Christianity, he
ought to have mentioned them; and,
to be sure, along with these, in this
most dangerous and difficult time, they
had an extraordinary assistance of the
Holy Spirit of God, to influence their
minds, and govern their practice. These
things, in justice to Christianity, he
ought to have produced: but instead
of

of that, the reader's attention is turned
off to two other caufes, which could be
of litttle or no benefit to this religion ;
indeed, the firft of them, a confidora-
ble prejudice to it, namely, repentance
for paft fins, and a laudable defire of
fupporting the fociety into which they
were entered. He here retails the malicious falfehoods which the Heathens
caft upon the Chriftians, of alluring
into their party the moft atrocious cri-
minals ; and adds, *Thofe perfons who
in the world had followed, though in an
imperfect manner, the dictates of benevo-
lence and propriety, derived fuch a calm
fatisfaction from the opinion of their
own rectitude, as rendered them much
lefs fufceptible of the fudden emotions of
fhame, of grief, and of terror, which
have given birth to fo many wonderful*

K 2   *converfions*

conversions.—Will not hope have some
effect upon a generous mind ? And must
not, then, the Christian assurance, given
to every virtuous person, of an endless
life, of inconceivable glory and happiness for ever in it, be more powerful
to persuade the good man to the embracing this religion, who had no alte-
ration to make in his practice, and must
have this self-satisfaction so prodigiously
increased, by knowing, that he hereby
had acquired the favour of his God,
and was certain of his protection and
blessing here, and his eternal reward
hereafter—must not these be more likely to work upon a virtuous and generous mind, than to be left totally desti-
tute of them ; and be, indeed, more
powerful to convert him, than the fear
of future punishment could be to any
profligate

profligate Heathens, which punifhment
they expected not, and were all taught
to defpife, and who, to become Chriftians, muft change the whole courfe of
their lives, get the better of long and
eftablifhed habits of vice, and ever after live in direct oppofition to all their
beloved lufts, paffions, interefts? Has
he, indeed, known many of thefe converfions in a Chriftian country, where
the motives to them are fo much more
powerful? If he has, his experience is
very different from that of all the reft
of mankind; and yet, upon this very
falfe fuppofition, he goes on to vilify
and abufe even our Saviour himfelf.

Page 573. *After the example of their*
Divine Mafter, the miffionaries of the
Gofpel difdained not the fociety of men,

K 3 *and*

and especially of women, oppreſſed by the conſciouſneſs, and very often by the effects, of their vices.—It is impoſſible that a man ſhould be a believer in Chriſt, or of any moderation in his infidel principles, who writes in this malevolent manner of the moſt holy, but compaſſionate Jeſus : for, was it not his cuſtom to preach in their ſynagogues every Sabbath-day, and in all places of the moſt public reſort, at their great feſtivals, and in their temple, and to the Scribes and Phariſees, and Jewiſh rulers ; *ſo that in ſecret he did nothing ?* And was not this alſo the practice of the Apoſtles ? What is it, then, which gives a pretence for this infamous ſcandal ? (Not to be warm upon ſuch an occaſion would be a fooliſh and criminal apathy.)   Why, Chriſt had ſome

women

women to attend him, one of whom had been a great finner; and he alſo tells the Phariſees, that he came " not to call the righteous but ſinners to repentance:"—a ſevere ſarcaſm this upon theſe hypocritical men, who were all abominably wicked, and yet gloried in their outward righteouſneſs; and a dreadful denunciation likewiſe againſt all thoſe, who, as men, muſt be ſinners, and, as infidels, almoſt always the greater ſinners, but who will yet refuſe to receive any atonement for ſin, or divine aſſiſtance againſt it, and will moſtly inſolently ſtand upon their own ſtrength and rectitude for acceptance and happineſs with the all-holy and juſt Governor and Judge of the world.

Moſt palpably miſtaken and unjuſt

is

is Mr. Gibbon, then, in this part of his cause of Christianity's progress ; and as to the care of the sect's reputation, this is such a poor motive to virtue, that I should never have thought it worthy of notice, if this gentleman had not made it so. Every sect has this motive, but every sect is not made virtuous by it ; nay, we know ourselves the very reverse to happen. Our infidels, as to number, are nothing, I thank God, in comparison of our Christians ; and do they therefore excel in righteousness ? We have also among us many sects of believers, and none of them are remarkable for their superior virtue, and some of them are infamous for a very different character : and if we will believe the primitive Christian writers, it was so in their time. But as Mr. Gibbon

bon will hardly allow them any credit, I will produce him two, which no Chris-tian can deny, Rev. ii. 6. *But this thou hast, that thou hatest the deeds of the Nicolaitanes, which I also hate ;* and 1 Theff. ii. 10, *Whose coming is with all deceivableness of unrighteousness ;* and one that he will not deny, namely, the bad character which these writers give of the Gnosticks, which, as these were Christians in name, and the scandal in-jured the Christians themselves, we may be sure that they would not have so openly confessed, was it a thing to be doubted of, or with truth to be denied. This charge against them Mr. Gibbon himself acknowledges ; but it is here worthy of notice, that he gives from them the same retort upon the church, and hereby contradicts himself, and ef-fectually

fectually deſtroys that very cauſe of Chriſtianity's growth, which he is here inſiſting upon.

The ſeverity of the then Chriſtian morals, ſet forth in ſo many pages, is a ſtill farther proof of the inſufficiency, and even falſeneſs, of this his pretended cauſe. The ſtate of perſecution to which the Chriſtians were then continually liable, and by which they frequently ſuffered, to the loſs of every thing dear to them, and the being afflicted with every thing that is miſerable in this life, made it moſt neceſſary for them to diſengage, as far as it was poſſible, their affections from this dangerous world ; and more eſpecially from the endearments of marriage, which muſt have proved a moſt violent temptation,

tation, and a dangerous fnare to them ǂ: fo violent indeed, that St. Paul advifes the Chriftians in thefe feafons to abftain from marriage : and the many idolatries practifed by the Heathens upon almoft every occafion, rendered it equally requifite that they fhould keep themfelves at a diftance from thofe offices which would entangle them in this great and juftly-abominated crime. Thefe, however, were not fo many as to render the Chriftians ufelefs to the commonwealth ; for we find many of them employed in many departments of it, which Mr. Gibbon feems to think inconfiftent with their religion, though, notwithftanding all their then ftrictnefs, it is certain that they did not. The firft Heathen convert to Chriftianity was, we know, a profelyte to the Jewifh religion,

gion, who muſt neceſſarily abhor and
avoid all idolatry ; and yet he was a
centurion in the Roman army.

Page 581. The fifth cauſe of the
growth of Chriſtianity, the active government of the church.

He here attributes a great deal of
the ſafety and aggrandizing of it to the
Chriſtian's ambition of raiſing themſelves to the offices of the church : but
the weakneſs, nay, the injuſtice, of this
cauſe, muſt appear, when it is confidered that all theſe offices were for life,
and could not be frequently filled ; that
not one in a thouſand could obtain any
one of them, nor in ten thouſand the
higheſt of them all ; that, when obtained, they did but ſubject the poſ-
ſeſſor

feffor to an excefs of trouble and danger, danger both of body and foul,
and, if there be any truth in Chriftian
hiftory, were, till near the clofe of
the third century, much more eagerly
fhunned, than fought for, by the Chriftian people.

As to the church government eftablifhed by the Apoftles, it is nothing to
our prefent purpofe ; and fo I pafs on
to page 586, where he makes the union
of the church one great caufe of its
growth : but had he given the real cafe
here, he would have fet it down, the
divifions and contefts of the church ;
and of thefe he himfelf has furnifhed
us with a good many inftances. This
would have been the juft reprefentation of the matter, but to do this
would

would have been to turn the caufe directly againſt his purpoſe ; and, therefore, the very reverſe is aſſerted by
him.

CHAP.

C H A P. IX.

PAGE 591. A community of goods was not adopted by the firſt Chriſtians in the manner he has ſtated it. The zeal of ſome drew them into this practice; but it was not required of any, it was voluntary in them all. St. Peter's words are, *While it remained with thee, was it not thine own, and after it was ſold, was it not in thine own power?* And even Mr. Gibbon's words are, " The converts were permitted to retain the poſſeſſion of their patrimony." It was, therefore, for the lie, and intended deceit, that Ananias and his wife were ſtruck dead; and thus the Scriptures declare it. He might, therefore, have

ſpared

spared the following innuendo, *that in hands less pure than those of the Apostles it might soon have been corrupted.* Never men shewed such an honest disregard to this world and all its interests as the Apostles did, their great Master excepted ; and even in this instance, we find them immediately casting away the care of this money from themselves, and putting it into other hands. But a reflection of this kind would be pleasing to many people, and beget a smile against the Apostles ; which was an advantage not to be lost.

It may, perhaps, be proper, also, to mention another instance which may seem to countenance Mr. Gibbon, although not noticed by him. Our Saviour required the young rich man to

sell

fell all that he had, and give to the poor, that he might become his difci-ple, and have treafure in heaven : but this was then neceffary, becaufe his reli-gion was to be for a long time in a moft dangerous and perfecuted condi-tion ; and if the man could not before-hand refolve to abandon his poffeffions, he could not remain a follower of Chrift, but muft afterwards apoftatize, to his greater condemnation and ruin.

That the charity of the Chriftians, in not only relieving their own poor, but many of the Heathen befides, and alfo in faving, and carefully breeding up, many of their children, whom their horrible and brutifh ignorance had ex-pofed to deftruction, muft have had a very beneficial effect for the Chriftian

L   religion,

religion, cannot be denied : but this belongs to, and ought to have been inserted in, his account of the fourth cause, the good lives of the Christians. Yet there it is not; and why so? Why it would, in that place, have done honour and service to their religion ; it is in this so introduced, as to be made a reproach and detriment to it. And here it ought to be noticed, that the then Christians, who were made so poor by Dr. Middleton, as to be unable to purchase a few copies of a small Apology, in defence of their lives, properties, and religion too, are found to be so rich in Mr. Gibbon, as to bribe over the Heathens to their party.—But I must mention another species of their charity, practised in Cyprian's time, which is not noticed by Mr. Gibbon : that when,

in

in a great plague which raged in Afri-
ca and Carthage, the nearest relations
fled from infected persons, and left
them to perish for want of assistance,
many of the Christians went to, and
took care of, those people, and saved
their lives; though, to be sure, often
with the loss of their own.

Page 597. Public pennance. Excom-
munication was ordered and practised
by St. Paul; and with excommunicated
persons the Christians were not so much
as to eat. It was the delivering the
unhappy person to Satan; who, according to the evil, malicious nature of apos-
tate spirits, was used most horribly to
torment the poor criminal, till, by his
being again restored to Christ, he was
delivered from Satan's power, and made

happy

happy in the favour and protection of his Saviour and his God, and in an affurance of pardon and everlasting happinefs in heaven :—a demonstration this of the neceffity, truth, benefit, of the Christian religion; and no wonder, then, that an exclusion from it was fo exceffively dreaded, and fo much endured by the penitent to have it taken off. But, certainly, this feverity of difcipline was more likely to hinder, than promote, a converfion to this faith. It laid thofe people under a moft violent temptation to abandon fuch a harfh religion as this; and, in cafe they had done it, we may be fure that the Heathens would have received them with the greateft cordiality ; and they could have nothing to dread from the refentment of their former friends. It cannot be doubted,

that

that the liberal alms of the Chriſtians
muſt have occaſioned ſome converſions
among the poor; but that merciful and
loving temper, which was enjoined even
to enemies, by this religion, muſt have
made a great many more, and thoſe of
the moſt virtuous and happy diſpoſitions. This is, indeed, an argument
ſtrong in Chriſtianity's favour, and we
do accept it from Mr. Gibbon with all
thankfulneſs, whatever his deſign was
in confeſſing it.

Page 602. We have, in this place,
ſuch expreſſions as only befit a Chriſtian; but it is impoſſible this author
ſhould be ſuch. The whole bent of
his ſoul appears to be ſet againſt Chriſtianity, and he ſees nothing in it, but
with that jaundiced eye which turns

every

every thing to its own blackneſs and
horror. And here he thinks his five
cauſes ſo powerful, that, inſtead of being ſurpriſed at the rapid progreſs of
Chriſtianity, his wonder is, that it was
not ſtill more univerſal and rapid. Let
us, then, more carefully examine this
matter; for to me this appears an eaſi-
neſs of belief greater than that with
which modern Deiſts are wont to reproach us Chriſtians, and ſadly ſhews,
to what an unreaſonable length a deep
prejudice can carry a bright and pene-
trating genius. I remember a learned
man, of theſe principles, to have doubted whether there ever had been ſuch a
perſon as Chriſt. But ſomething of
this kind was neceſſary to be done, in
order to take off, if poſſible, one of
our arguments, thoroughly enforced by
Mr.

Mr. Jenyns, for the truth of Christianity, namely, the greatness of its growth,
when the cause, and the propagators of
it, were naturally so unfit to produce
such a wonderful effect.

L 4 CHAP.

CHAP. X.

WHEN Chrift Jefus was going to die for the falvation of the world, he tells his Apoftles, that before the deftruction of Jerufalem, not then 40 years diftant, *this Gofpel of the kingdom fhalt be preached in all the world*; (and St. Paul tells us it was fo within 30 years;) and, from the parable of the leaven, and the grain of muftard-feed, forefhews the prodigious encreafe of it:—ftrangely, but moft furely prophetic this denunciation, when his religion, and the means to effect it, were both of them of such an unpromifing nature; when there was nothing to propagate it, but the preachings of twelve illiterate fifher-men,

men, who were equally deſtitute of
learning, addreſs, or eloquence; and
who were to wander about the world
with this ſeemingly ſilly tale in their
mouths, that one Jeſus, who was by
his countrymen, the Jews, put to the
moſt cruel death, for being the vileſt
of malefactors, was riſen from the dead,
and become the Saviour of the world;
that he had commiſſioned, and ſent
them out to tell all mankind, that they
muſt believe in him and the one true
God, repent of all their ſins, abandon
every vice, and practiſe every virtue;
that they muſt reſiſt and abhor the religions of the ſeveral countries in which
they had been educated, and to which
they were moſt deeply prejudiced; give
up all the goods of this life, and en-
dure every thing miſerable in it, even
to

to the moſt torturous of deaths, which they muſt ſurely expect; and all for the ſake of this new religion, and the happineſs which it promiſed in a future life. Theſe were the men our Saviour ſent out to propagate his religion, and this was the work he had given them to do : and very ſtrange it is, that he ſhould know them ſo thoroughly, as to think, nay, be ſure of it too, that they would meddle in ſuch an undertaking, and, much more, perſevere in it; and ſtranger ſtill, that theſe miſſionaries ſhould be able to convert the moſt powerful, knowing, and poliſhed nation that ever was in the world, convert them from that ancient religion of theirs, which had all their luſts, prejudices, paſſions, gratifications, and worldly intereſts, to attach them to it; which

had

had all the wit of their philosophers, all the learning and power of the world to defend it; to which religion they attributed the growth and prosperity of their mighty empire, and to the abandoning of which, by the Christians, they imputed every calamity which befel them after the rise of the new religion; and *that*, therefore, they treated with all the abuse, hatred, persecution, which malice so powerfully urged on could inspire, and which Christ so justly and particularly foretold to his Apostles when he was sending them out.

By these means, and in this manner, and against such an opposition, was Christianity to be propagated; and let any man of the least impartiality say, whether it was possible for the Apostles

to

to have any fuccefs in this work, unlefs
favoured with that high and miraculous
interpofition of God which the New
Teftament gives an account of, and
which it is Mr. Gibbon's intention to
deny, and his endeavour totally to deftroy; and, along with this, an infpiration and divine influence of the
Holy Ghoft, to work upon the minds
of the hearers, and give them that in-
genuoufnefs of heart which fhould caufe
them to attend to, and be convinced by,
their preaching and miracles. This moft
important period, upon which all future
proceedings of the Chriftians did entirely depend, is paffed over without notice by Mr. Gibbon: and if truth was
to be thrown out of the cafe, and he
had nothing more to regard than the
credit of his underftanding, he would
have

have been very wife in this proceeding:
for although it be certain that he no
more believes the miracles of Chrift
and his Apoftles than thofe of the af-
ter-Chriftians, yet to have at once condemned the former would have given
fuch difguft to many, would fo clearly
have fhewn the impoffibility of the
Apoftles fucceeding in this work, and
have expofed him to fuch a certain confutation, that it was not a thing to be
undertaken. He would have been dif-
proved by the very exiftence of fuch a
book as the New Teftament. He was,
therefore, neceffitated to take up Chriftianity at a later date, when, from its
being very generally propagated and
well eftablifhed in many places, he could,
with the greater plaufibility, afcribe its
wonderful growth to the five caufes he
has

has affigned for it. But then, it is to be obferved, that, as thefe will not at all relate to the firft planting of Chriftianity, they are indeed totally befide his purpofe, and prove nothing at all for him. Let us, however, go on to confider them as he has been pleafed to ftate them; and here we fhall not find him to fucceed, but to be palpably defeated in his attempt, although he has, by the moft partial calculations, endeavoured to leffen the progrefs of this religion. That they would, if juftly fet down, be of confiderable effect, is not to be denied; but, as in this light they would all of them have given moft convincing proofs of Chriftianity's truth, he has been compelled, in order to avoid this confequence, fo to pervert them, as in all of them to leffen, and

moft

most of them to annihilate their whole
force, and, in some instances, to turn
them to the destruction of his own intended proof.

If he had said, that Christianity, by
ascertaining and opening the being and
nature of God, and shewing him to
be the Creator, Sustainer, and Moral
Governor of the world, who had a regard to the behaviour of his moral
creatures, and would reward or punish
them as they should deserve, and by
these means merited from all rational
creatures, capable of knowing him, such
a high homage of adoration, suitable to
his holiness, justice, goodness, and infinite power, as made it peculiar to him ;
and that this religion, by prescribing
and making known such a spiritual devotion

votion as was fitting for man to give,
and the Divine Being to receive, and
by procuring for us sinners, and our
imperfect and worthless services, an acceptance from his infinite purity and
justice—if he had said, that Christianity
by these means did render itself so exceedingly reasonable, amiable, and beneficial, that it ought to have drawn
over every sensible person to the embracing of it, and more especially so
when set in opposition to the impure,
abominable, superstition of the Heathens—(and in so saying he would have
done no more than justice to our religion)—if he had said this, he then, indeed, had given a cause which must
have been of great force for the promotion of Christianity. But as this
would have been so convincing an argument

gument of its goodnefs and truth, he
was compelled to evade it; and he has,
by making nothing of divine worfhip,
and by blaming the primitive Chriftians
for their refufal to give any to the Heathen gods, not only deftroyed the force
of his own caufe, but manifeftly turned it againft himfelf: for fuch an unreafonable, obftinate denial in the Chriftians to do what was innocent in his
eyes, and meritorious in that of the
Pagans, could not fail of breeding in
the latter fuch an hatred to the Chriftians, and fuch a wide feparation between them, as muft have proved a very
great detriment, inftead of any advantage, to the Chriftian caufe. Every one
at all acquainted with mankind, knows
that it is not an unreafonable, perverfe
oppofition to their wills, but an eafy

M   com-

compliance with them as far as we can, which will beſt gain upon the underſtanding, and ſo win over their hearts as to render them moſt ſuſceptible of conviction.

The ſame, alſo, is to be obſerved of his ſecond cauſe: The immortality of the ſoul, and the retributions of a future life.—If he had ſaid, and in juſtice to Chriſtianity he ought to have ſaid, that the nature of God and man was ſuch as to make man deſerve and expect a future life of retribution; that Chriſtianity did, by giving us a certainty of this future life in an infinitely more perfect exiſtence, and for ever enjoying in it an inconceivable degree of glory and happineſs, which happineſs every man muſt wiſh for, and this religion has enſured

enfured to every virtuous perfon upon
the reafonable and eafy terms of the
Gofpel, but which had been banifhed
from the Heathen world by their abfurd notions of this future life, and retributions of it, as alfo by the falfe reafonings of their philofophers upon this
moft important fubject ; if he had faid,
that thefe Chriftian difcoveries contributed to the growth of this religion, he
would have offered a caufe which had
real weight in it, and muft be very
powerful for his purpofe. But as a moft
material proof would have from hence
refulted to Chriftianity, he was neceffitated to turn off the reader's attenrion
from it, and fix his mind upon other
matters ; namely, the falfe expectation
of a judgment immediately to come, of
an earthly millennium, of the confla-

M 2   gration

gration of Rome and this world ; and to
an excefs of threatening and fear, which
the wifeft of the Heathens all defpifed,
and which muft render this caufe of
very little, if indeed of any effect at
all, to the promoting Chriftianity : and
to compleat the deftruction of it, he
ridicules the prophetic language in the
Scriptures, of the gold and precious
ftones wherewith the New Jerufalem was
to be built ; and thus deftroying the
credit of thofe writings, which, by his
own confeffion, do alone infure this immortality to us, he annihilates his fecond
caufe.

Third caufe : The miracles of the
primitive Chriftians—Had he declared,
that, although all miracles had ceafed
with the lives of the Apoftles, yet was
there

there fo authentic a teftimony left of
them in the Scripture, that there could
be no reafonable doubt entertained of
them, he then would have given a
caufe moft powerful indeed for the
promotion of Chriftianity : and, befides, had he farther confeffed, that there
were fome remains of the fame miraculous powers continued in the church to
the 2d and 3d centuries, to teftify for
Chrift's religion, he would have added
force to his caufe, and demonftrated
its truth and tendency to propagate
and encreafe that religion. But as
this was a thing not to be done by
him, he has artfully turned off the
whole into an infpiration falfe and ridiculous, faid many things fubverfive of
all miracles, and made plaufible impof-
tures of all thofe which the primitive
Chriftians afferted of themfelves; and

M 3   he

he has hereby not only ruined his de-
fign, but turned his own caufe againft
himfelf: for this falfe pretence to miracles would only have put them upon
a level with the Heathens, who frequently afcribed the fame power to
their Gods; fo that little good could
have arifen from this pretence to the
Chriftians: but if their impofture had
been difcovered, as certainly it muft
have been in a Heathen government,
and with fuch a majority of the people, and they all fo eager, againft
them, it muft have torn up Chriftianity
by the roots, and entirely extirpated it.
Thofe people, who were fuch bitter
enemies to the Chriftians, as to load
their religion and them with the horrid
and unjuft calumnies of worfhipping
an afs's head, killing and devouring
children, and ufing promifcuous copu-
lations,

lations, would have blazed this matter abroad, to their total fubverfion. But fo palpably different was the cafe here, that thofe miraculous powers which Mr. Gibbon fo ftrenuoufly denies, were then acknowledged by the Heathens themfelves, though under the name of magick, by which they rendered them not only ufelefs, but even pernicious, to Chriftianity.

Fourth caufe: The virtue of the primitive Chriftians.—We have an odd contraft here: the impofture and villainy of thefe people were Mr. Gibbon's 3d caufe; their integrity and virtue are, in this inftance, to conftitute his 4th caufe. But paffing this over, I am to obferve, that, if he had, as in juftice to Chriftianity he ought to have

M 4   done,

done, set down, as a cause, the manifest truth and purity of the Christian morality, and the strong motives
it held out to virtue, which were infinitely more powerful than the world
ever before knew, and these suitably
acknowledged by a superior purity and
goodness of life in the Christians, which
must have drawn upon them and their
religion the esteem of every virtuous
and sensible person, (and sometimes he
finds occasion to speak of Christianity
in this manner,) he then would have
produced a cause most justly and greatly operating in Christianity's growth.
But as a representation of this kind
would have been too favourable for
this religion, he is forced to suppress it,
and to substitute in its place that ex-
cessive severity of life and doctrine into
which

which those miserable times of persecution had, driven the oppressed Christians; and has thereby destroyed the intended effect of his own cause, and turned it against himself : for that rigidness and severity of living which was then required of every believer in Christ, must have been very discouraging, and greatly obstructed, instead of promoting a conversion to this faith. It is not a very easy matter to persuade a great number of people to embrace such a severe and miserable austerity of life as he has here spoken of.

As to his 5th cause, that, if justly given, would have been of some advantage to Christianity ; but it is surprising how he could fall into such a palpable mistake, as to make the union of the

church

church any help to its spreading, when
there was nothing but dissention, and
the moft rancorous divisions, among
them. The apoftolical writings shew
us, that this was the cafe with them
even in the firft century, whilft the
Apoftles were alive, and miraculous
power and divine infpiration were common in the church ; (fo unwilling are
men to give up their own prejudices to
any conviction whatfoever !) and the
Chriftian writers, afterwards, shew that
this was the cafe with them in the 2d
and 3d centuries : but in the 4th, when
Paganifm was brought to its expiring
gafp, the controverfy between the Trinitarians and the followers of Arius,
raifed fuch a flame in the church, and
bred fuch animofities between the con-
tending parties, as made them the deri-
sion

fion and fport even of the Heathens themfelves. Thefe are inconteftible facts, and will hereafter be fully proved even by Mr. Gibbon himfelf ; and therefore this moft learned writer was ftrangely. miftaken when he made the union of the church one caufe of its prodigious en-creafe. Let us not, however, at the prefent, give up this difpute ; but, for the reader's more perfect fatisfaction, let us go on to examine the heads of this caufe, as he is pleafed to fet them down in his book.

The active government of the church, the primitive freedom and equality, the inftitutions of bifhops and prefbyters and of provincial councils, the progrefs of the epifcopal authority, the metropo-litans, the ambition of the Roman Pon-tiff,

tiff, the diſtinction of laity and clergy, theſe are (to ſtop for a while) made by him a principal means of Chriſtianity's wonderful growth ; but how either one, or all of theſe put together, ſhould have any conſiderable effect in the converſion of the Heathens, I ſee not, nor do I believe that any impartial, conſiderate perſon will ſee. If ſuch a government as this had been peculiar to the Chriſtians, it muſt have proved of ſome benefit to their religion ; but where is the civilized nation that is deſtitute of it ? It is certain that the Romans were not, and that they had all the advantages which could poſſibly ariſe from any of theſe inſtitutions in the greateſt perfection ; truly in much greater perfection than the Chriſtians did, or could poſſibly, poſſeſs. It is eaſy to diſcern
that

that some policy of this kind was absolutely neceſſary to the exiſtence of Chriſtianity ; but how this little weak government of the little weak church,
without any other ſupport than what
conſcience could give it, ſhould enable
theſe few religioniſts not only to reſiſt,
but prevail againſt, that policy which
was ſo firmly eſtabliſhed, and had all
the encouragement that law, power,
learning, prejudice, wickedneſs, the
moſt dreadful puniſhments, and the moſt
ample rewards, could give it, I cannot diſcover, although I have given it
the moſt careful conſideration. Hitherto, then, his own cauſe militates againſt
himſelf : but he alſo adds, the obla-
tions and revenues of the churches, and
the diſtribution of them, excommunica-
tion, public pennance, and the dignity
of

of the epifcopal government. To thefe
I anfwer, That to make excommunica-
tion and pennance, which were fo exceffively fevere againft all apoftacy from
the faith, or any wickednefs in it after
its reception, a caufe of Chriftianity's
growth, is ftrange indeed; he fhould
have fet them down as a great obftruc-
tion to it. The dignity of the bifhops,
and the revenues of the churches, were
certainly as nothing in comparifon of
the Roman magiftracy, wealth, and
power; and the very frequent and mi-
ferable perfecutions by which the Chriftians often fuffered, and to which they
were continually expofed, muft have rendered thefe advantages of ftill lefs effi-
cacy to Mr. Gibbon's purpofe,—muft, in
fact, have turned them entirely againft
it. That love of the world, which alone
could

could have given them any force with the Chriftians, muft have caft them off from Chriftianity, and made Heathens of them all.

Upon the whole of this matter, then, we find this ingenious writer to be very unfortunate in the caufes he has affign-ed for the growth of fuch a religion as Chriftianity. They are all wrongly ftated ; they are all ineffectual for his purpofe ; and in many inftances directly make againft it.

CHAP.

C H A P. XI.

THERE are some other reasons afterwards offered by him, which, it must be confessed, would have been of advantage to this religion, if properly stated ; namely, the philosophers seeing the folly of Heathenism, the incredulity and ridicule of the learned, and of the priests themselves who officiated in their religious services, and the great scepticism which these things produced among many of their people. It is certain that there is strength in these causes, and that in such a state of things they must have been very considerable helps to Christianity ; so considerable, indeed, that they seem to have affected Mr. Gib-

bon

bon himfelf, and for a while to have made a convert of him. His words are, *Some deities of a more fafhionable caft, might have occupied the deferted temples of Jupiter and Apollo, if, in the decifive moment, the wifdom of Providence had not interpofed a genuine revelation, fitted to infpire the moft rational efteem and conviction, whilft, at the fame time, it was adorned with all that could attract the curiofity, the wonder, the veneration, of the people.*

How to reconcile this to the whole tenour of his book, and many of his direct expreffions, I know not. Muft not both Chrift and his Apoftles have been, according to him, a fet of the moft profligate deceivers? And are thefe the people who brought down this

N   genuine

genuine and amiable revelation from heaven ? This is ftrange indeed ! Nor can I fee how he can reconcile it to the character of his moft highly efteemed and commended hiftorian Tacitus, who, in his own tranflation, ufes thefe words of the Chriftians and their religion : *Branded with deferved infamy, a dire fuperftition was even introduced to Rome itfelf, which receives and protects whatever is atrocious ; they were all convicted, not fo much for the crime of fetting fire to the city, as for their hatred of mankind :*—in which words, befides the manifeft and fpiteful falfity of them, and the direct contradiction given to Mr. Gibbon himfelf in the above-cited paffage, it might eafily be fhewn, were it worth infifting upon, that he has made his tranflation worfe than the original,

'ginal, in order to throw an odium upon
Chriftianity. And as to its being fitted
to attract the curiofity, wonder, and veneration of the people, this will not, I
fuppofe, be accounted a reproach to it :
and how, indeed, could it be otherwife,
when it was to open to us the nature
of the One Infinite Being, and the moft
ftupendous of all his wonderful providences ;—providences, which the angels
defire to look into, and which were to
be the moft expreffive of, and honourable to, his infinite nature, that he
would ever fhew for the good of his
creatures.

But it is proper that we fhould enquire into thofe particulars which have
given him fuch a high notion of the
eafinefs of Chriftianity's fuccefs. They

are

are set down, pages 601-2 : *The fashion
of incredulity was communicated from
the philosopher to the man of pleasure
or business, from the noble to the ple-
beian, and from the master to the menial
slave who waited at his table, and who
eagerly listened to the freedom of his con-
versation. On public occasions the philo-
sophical part of mankind affected to treat
with respect and decency the religious in-
stitutions of their country; but their
secret contempt penetrated through the
thin and awkward disguise : and even
the people, when they discovered that
their deities were rejected and derided by
those whose rank and understanding they
were accustomed to reverence, were filled
with doubts and apprehensions concerning the truth of those doctrines to which
they had yielded a most implicit belief.*

The

*The decline of ancient prejudice expofed
a very numerous portion of human-kind
to the danger of a painful and comfort-
lefs fituation. A ftate of fcepticifm and
fufpence may amufe a few inquifitive
minds. But the practice of fuperftition
is fo congenial to the multitude, that, if
they are forcibly awakened, they ftill re-
gret the lofs of their pleafing vifion.
Their love of the marvellous and fuper-
natural, their curiofity with regard to
future events, and their ftrong propenfity
to extend their hopes and fears beyond the
limits of the vifible world, were the principal caufes which favoured the eftablifhment of polytheifm. So urgent on the vul-
gar is the neceffity of believing, that the fall
of any fyftem of mythology will moft probably be fucceeded by the introduction of
fome other mode of fuperftition.* And fo he

N 2 goes

goes on, in the words already quoted, to
wonder that the progress of Christianity
was not, in these circumstances, still
more rapid and universal. We must,
then, examine this matter, as laid down
by him.

Mr. Gibbon dates this scepticism from
the rise of Christianity to the extinction of Heathenism; but, upon enquiry, we shall not find this assertion ve-
rified, but falsified, by stubborn facts.
The philosophers, indeed, denied all
futurity, and derided the Heathen notion of retribution there; but we do
not find them in any readiness, nor
the people either, to give up their old
religion, but, on the contrary, tenaci-
ous, persevering, obstinate, in the defence of it, and doing all that power,
malice,

malice, falsehood, genius, learning, could
do, for the support of it. Thus we
have seen it to be with his favourite his-
torian Tacitus; and this is abundantly
proved by Christianity's not being able
to prevail for a hundred years together,
and till Heathen Rome had become
Christian, under the authority of Con-
stantine the Great : it is, besides, proved,
by the many and cruel persecutions in-
flicted upon the Christians during this
time ; by the cries of the people, upon
every occasion, to have the Christians
given to the lions ; and by the defence
acknowledged by Mr. Gibbon to be
made for Heathenism by the philosophers of the second and third centuries.
He is, therefore, most shamefully mistaken in that state of the case which he
has given, and upon which he hath so

N 4   con-

confidently founded Chriftianity's fuccefs. And if any one be defirous to fee
this fact undoubtedly confirmed, I refer
him to Vol. I. chap. 16, of the late
Dr. Leland's Advantages and Neceffity
of the Chriftian Revelation, where he
will receive entire fatisfaction on this
point : only, as this truly learned and
great man hath not mentioned Plutarch
among his Heathen authorities, I will
obferve, that this philofopher, in ac-
counting for the ceffation of oracles
among the Heathens by the fuppofed
death of the dæmons who gave them,
and who, though very long lived, might
not be immortal, and by his endeavouring to explain away, and account for,
the monftrous idolatry of the Egyptians,
gives me a ftrong fufpicion that he
knew of Chriftianity, and took thefe
methods

thods to preferve that moſt abſurd and
bloody ſuperſtition from being deſtroyed
by the reaſonableneſs, purity, and truth,
of the Chriſtian religion. And I muſt,
alſo, for the ſame purpoſe, mention that
great genius, and learned philoſopher,
Longinus, who ſhews himſelf to be
well acquainted, both with Judaiſm and
Chriſtianity; and yet, what concern
does he expreſs at Homer's battle of
the Heathen gods! And what care
does he take to hinder it from hurting
their religion!

It is true, that there was a Lucian
in the ſecond century, who did moſt ſe-
verely ridicule the Heathen ſuperſtition;
but then he did ſo to Chriſtianity as
well as to that, and, indeed, to all religion along with them; and is, therefore,

fore, nothing to Mr. Gibbon's purpofe.
And it is alfo true, that Seneca, in the
firft century, fpoke very harfhly of the
Heathen worfhip ; but then it is equally
true, that he advifes the people to conform to it. But although erroneous in
this his ftate of the cafe, Mr. Gibbon
is not fo as to the confequences which
muft follow from fuch a freedom of con-
verfation, and much more from fuch an
infidel freedom of writing as he has affumed.

It is his opinion, and certainly the
truth, that the people will have fome
religion or other. Man's nature requires
it ; and this natural inclination, as well
as the reafon of the thing, is a demonftration, that it is natural to man, and
ought to be received by every one of
this

this nature, and muft be, and will be
fo, if he be not debafed to the loweft
degree of wickednefs and wrong judgment. And now, from his own mouth,
I befeech Mr. Gibbon to confider what
he has been doing in this his attempt
to deftroy Chriftianity ; and whether
the world will owe him any thanks for
it, even if there was not to be a future
life after the prefent, or any retribution
in it. Can he find any other religion
upon earth fo good for us as that of
Chrift, which he has but juft now juftly
defcribed to be " a genuine revelation,
fitted to infpire the moft rational efteem
and conviction ?" Can he find any fo
good as this, and that as it is taught in
his own national church, for the reafonablenefs, purity, and ufefulnefs of its
precepts, and for its moft powerful en-
forcements

forcements of virtue?—And can he avoid feeing the dreadful confequences which muft follow from its being deftroyed? for which he has, however, fo heartily laboured, and which will not be without its effect (I pray God, that it may be but little) upon a now luxurious, carelefs, and very profligate people. Poffibly he may need to be told, but the reader certainly ought to be told, the dreadful confequences of it.

Thefe writings of his will propagate fceptifm and infidelity, by a great deal already too rife among us; thefe a total difrelifh to, and breach of every virtue; thefe a hatred of all the fanctions, which enforce virtue and reftrain from vice; thefe the keeneft hatred of the Gofpel, and every thing enjoined by it; and thefe an increafe and inundation of wicked-

wickednefs, till it produces a total dif-
regard to the welfare of the ftate, great
mifchief to it, and to all the individuals
of it, and till it fhall at laft throw it
into flavery, and all the abfurdities, fuperftition, and idolatry of the church of
Rome, from which we have, by our
Reformation, been fo long and fo hap-
pily emancipated : for then the bafenefs of the people's minds will make
them require the iron hand of arbitrary
power to controul their pernicioufnefs,
will render their remains of liberty but
a curfe to them, and themfelves, therefore, not only unwilling to defend, but
eager to give it up ; and this bafenefs
will make their minds fo connatural to
the bafenefs and fuperftition of Popery,
that they will be ready to abandon their
own true and holy belief, and eager to
accept of the outward fervices, the con-
jurations,

jurations, and the absolutions of the church of Rome. And thus shall our true and spiritual religion, the boast of Christianity, and our free and happy constitution, the admiration and envy of every sensible and virtuous man, be totally destroyed from among us; and this, not only by the just judgment of an offended God, but by the natural effects of the things themselves:—an event so certain to follow from the increase of infidelity, that he must either wish for it, or be judicially blinded, who does not discern it, and from hence see the encreasing danger of our countries at this time.

Mr. Gibbon ought, therefore, out of love to the truth, to the welfare of mankind, and the good of his own country, to have struck out those parts of his

his book which are so hurtful to Christianity. Dr. Watson, in my opinion, yields a great deal too much to our Deists, when he allows that the usefulness and benefits of Christianity are no sure evidence of the truth of this religion: for as the Divine Being is infinitely good, and this his goodness was the cause of all creation; so it can never be, that the thing which is absolutely and entirely good, can be false—it must proceed from Him who is entire goodness and truth. And although we may, in other instances, be easily mistaken, yet not so in this of Christianity: it is so highly necessary to our welfare, both here and hereafter, indeed absolutely so, and so perfective of our nature, and surely productive of happiness, both in this and in the other world, that it must be true.

CHAP.

C H A P. XII.

PAGE 602. It is said, that the conquests of Rome paved the way for the conquests of Christianity. The assertion is true, and most highly honourable to this religion; because, as Rome civilized, and made its people thoughtful and intelligent, it shewed that Christianity is of such a nature, as to prevail where the people are most fitted to reason, to enquire, and to understand: and for want of this among the savages of America, our religion, to this hour, has not been able to make any considerable progress there.

That the Jews were so incredulous to the miracles of the divine prophet,

as to render it unneceffary to publifh any
Hebrew Gofpel, is a great miftake;
but fhews plainly what this gentleman
thinks, and would have his readers
think, of the miracles of Chrift and
his Apoftles. Acts ii. 41, we find 3000
converted by one preaching and the
miracle preceding it. Acts iv. 5000
converted by another preaching. Acts
v. 14, it is, " And believers were the
more added to the Lord, multitudes
both of men and women." Acts vi. 7,
it is, " And the word of God increafed,
and the number of the difciples multipli-
ed in Jerufalem greatly, and a great company of the priefts were obedient to
the faith." And Acts xxi. 20, James,
who then prefided over and governed the
church of Jerufalem, declares, " Thou
feeft, brother, how many thoufands of

Jews

Jews there are who believe :"—the original is, myriads or ten thoufands. It is, then, a miftake in this learned man to make the Jews fo incredulous to the Chriftian miracles : and he muft, confequently, be miftaken in the reafon he has affigned for there never having been a Hebrew Gofpel ; which, although the thing be doubtful, I do not believe there really ever was. The caufe of this is, however, eafily difcerned. There was one or more of the Apoftles always refiding at Jerufalem (to which place the neceffity of a Hebrew Gofpel was confined), till they were all killed, or had fled from it at the approach of that Roman war which deftroyed Jerufalem, the temple and public worfhip, and all the Jewifh legal rites ; and from his mouth, and the teachers authorized by him,

him, the Jews muſt have had ſuch a
full information of every thing in Chriſtianity, as rendered it unneceſſary for
them to have any Goſpel in writing.
And here I muſt obſerve, that, as the
Jewiſh teachers then did, as the church
of Rome now does, aſſume to themſelves an infallibility in interpreting their
Scriptures, and had, in faďt, to make
good this claim, texts by a great many
more numerous and forcible than Rome
can produce for herſelf; as their people were ſo long uſed to allow them this
high prerogative; and as theſe rulers
did almoſt all of them, in their con-
junďt body, deny and rejeďt Chriſt;—
conſidering theſe things, it is really wonderful how Chriſtianity could make any
progreſs at all among them; and it is
hence fully ſhewn, that the miracles

wrought

wrought for confirmation of it, must
have been stupendous and convincing
indeed. It is observed by Dr. Middleton's antagonists, that, according to his
own Introduction, he ought to have
begun his Enquiry with an examination
of the miracles of the first century, as
set forth in the New Testament, and
have shewn why and when the power of
working them ceased in the church;
but, instead of this fair proceeding, he
begins his Enquiry with those of the
fourth century, when the necessity of
them was nearly superseded ; when the
morals of the Christians were exceedingly corrupted by the outward peace
and prosperity of the church, and more
especially by the animosities and violent
contentions raised by the Arians against
the Trinitarians, which made some of
each

each fide ready to forge miracles for the
fupport of their different tenets, and the
willing and credulous people too ready
to receive them ; when, too, their love
of monkery, and the faints and their
rotten relicks, greatly hurt the purity
of their faith even in that century, but
in the next threw them into downright
fuperftition and idolatry. This is the
time in which Dr. Middleton chofe to
begin his Enquiry, afcending afterwards
to the third and fecond centuries ; and
in this he has been very nearly followed
by Mr. Gibbon. The miracles of the
third and fecond centuries are firft condemned by the latter ; and when he
thinks he has brought thofe into contempt, the miracles of Chrift and his
Apoftles are likewife attacked by him ;
and although in a covert, yet in a

moft

moſt pointed manner. To have begun
with thoſe of Chriſt and his immediate
followers, would have been an enterprize
too dangerous and offenſive. It was,
therefore, his moſt ſucceſsful method,
at firſt, to diſpute thoſe of a later time,
which could not be ſo certainly proved,
and would not give ſo great an offence ;
and then, as ſoon as the reader's mind
was ſufficiently prejudiced, he might
deny them all in general, when ſuch
condemnation would be the more eaſily
ſwallowed, and any hints taken which
might deſtroy the belief of them.

I do not ſay that this was the real deſign of Mr. Gibbon ; but I muſt affirm, that his proceeding thus was ſo
well fitted to produce theſe effects, that
he, who would defend the truth, ought

not

not to let it pass without notice. Self-
deceit is the easiest of all others, and
where there is any prejudice in the
mind, it is the most difficult to be
avoided: and if ever man was prejudiced against any thing, Mr. Gibbon
is, and most deeply so, against Christianity; for he sees nothing belonging
to it in a just, but distorted light, and
this has drawn him here into palpable
self - contradiction. He repeatedly allows a strong internal evidence to be in
Christianity, and yet in this place he
effectually destroys it. He will not allow the primitive Christian writers to
have offered any reason for their religion which was fitted to move a sensible man; and yet their principal defence of it was, the strong internal
evidence with which it abounded. They

not

not only expofed the abfurdity, falfehood, wickednefs, of Heathenifm ; but
they dwelt, and chiefly too, upon the
infinite benefit which Scripture inftruc-
tion had done, in opening and afcer-
taining the being and nature of God,
his creation of the world, his moral
government and providence over it, the
pure worfhip by which he is to be
ferved, his obfervance of, and regard
to, the moral behaviour of every man,
and his having appointed a day in which
he will judge the whole world in righte-
oufnefs, and reward or punifh every
man with an eternity of the greateft
happinefs or mifery, according to his
good or evil behaviour in this life ; by
his giving us a perfect rule of duty,
which forbids even the leaft vice, and
enjoins the moft perfect virtue and purity

rity of life ; purity, not only in our outward words and actions, but inwardly in our moſt ſecret thoughts and inclinations : and all this, as we hope to eſcape this moſt horrid and threatened miſery, and obtain this promiſed and moſt glorious happineſs. And is there, indeed, nothing which can convince in all theſe things ; and this, too, when they are ſet in oppoſition to the monſtrous corruptions and errors of Heatheniſm ? Mr. Gibbon does, in effect, affirm that there is not ; but at the ſame time he equally contradicts reaſon, and his own previous declaration. And here it muſt be obſerved, that, as he makes nothing at all of prophecy, utterly denies all miracles, and in this place deſtroys all internal evidence of Chriſtianity, he does, indeed, hereby effectually render it, as he here
would

would have it, unworthy the reception of any fensible man : but then we have fhewn him to be miftaken in every one of thefe inftances, and even to contradict himfelf.

As to the proportion of the Chriftians to that of the Heathens, it is of but fmall confequence ; and therefore I pafs it over, and proceed to page 613, where it is faid, that *the new sect of Chriftians was almost entirely composed of the dregs of the populace, of peasants and mechanics, of boys and women, of beggars and flaves, the last of whom might sometimes introduce the missionaries into the rich and noble families to which they belonged. These obscure teachers . . . . whilst they cautiously avoid the dangerous encounter of philosophers, mingle with the rude and illiterate crowd, and insinuate*

*infinuate themselves into thofe minds,
whom their age, their fex, or their edu-
cation, has the beft difpofed to receive
the impreffion of fuperftitious terrors:*
and this picture, although confeffed to
be an enemy's exaggeration, is yet declared not to be void of a faint refem-
blance.—That the majority of every
religion muft be made up of the populace, is unqueftionable; but that the
Chriftians were not entirely compofed
of them, but had many of ftation and
learning among them, is certain from
Pliny's letter to Trajan, as well as from
all the Chriftian apologifts. Had it,
however, been as it is here reprefented,
are we to be governed by the fafhion
of the world, or the reafonablenefs of
the thing? Can Mr. Gibbon think
that the writing in this manner will
do honour either to himfelf or to his
cauſe?

cauſe ? As to the Chriſtians avoiding
to encounter with the Heathen philoſophers, what can Mr. Gibbon intend by
ſuch an expreſſion ? Were not many of
the then Chriſtians philoſophers, and
men of deep learning ; and were they
not ſpoken to, and converted by, the
Chriſtians ? Is Heatheniſm, indeed, the
religion which the philoſophers profeſſ-
ed, and endeavoured to defend, to be
in reaſon preferred before Chriſtianity ?
And is the latter found to be unable to
defend itſelf in the opinion of rational
people ? It cannot be affirmed : the
very reverſe is but now aſſerted by Mr.
Gibbon himſelf ; and he muſt know
that the moſt learned and worthy men
of our nation, men who have done the
higheſt honour to it by their genius,
knowledge, virtue, have been ſtaunch
believers ; and of how different a character

racter from them the heads of our unbelievers have been, the world need
not be told from me.

Page 614.—It is a moft certain fact,
that almoft all herefies have arifen in
the church of Chrift from men's giving
too much deference to their own weak
reafon, and too little to the revelation
of an all-knowing and infinite God ;
and never was any fault more rife in
the world, than this at prefent is among
our people.

Page 614, 615.—It is acknowledged,
but with reftrictions, that there were
many perfons of rank and learning at
that time profeffing Chriftianity, though
thefe too few to take off entirely the
imputation of ignorance and obfcurity :
—but

but this, he allows, does, after all, give us the more reason to admire the merit and fuccefs of the Chriftians.—— He alfo fays, that, while Chriftianity promifes a heaven to the poor in fpirit, and the afflicted chearfully liften to it, the fortunate are fatisfied with the happinefs of this world.——That they are ever endeavouring to make themfelves fo, is allowed ; but that they are able to accomplifh their purpofe, I abfolutely deny : and the continued, various, and ruinous purfuits of thofe who are higheft in the world, confirm this to be the truth, as well as the confeffions at laft made by themfelves, and by the great Solomon.   And, indeed, the cleareft reafons, as well as the conftant experience of all mankind, fhews us it ever muft be fo.

Man

Man can never be gratified by the
pleasures of sense ; because sense is but
one, and the lowest, part of him. His
highest faculties are those of reason and
morality, from which must man's chief
happiness ever arise ; but whereof he
has such an imperfect use in this world,
that they can never satisfy him : and,
to aggravate his misfortune, man is
ever found to sacrifice the pleasures of
these to the lower and baser pleasures of
sense. Besides, Mr. Gibbon allows that
man is made for a future life ; and if
he be, what shall we say to the folly
and baseness of him, who, in opposition to this most exalted prerogative,
the end of his own nature, and the intention of his most beneficent Creator,
shall endeavour to pin himself down,
and give up all his affection and care,
to

to this infignificant world ; and this, to
the total neglect of that infinitely important futurity, wherein fuch neglect
muft prove his certain and everlafting
deftruction ?—Is it any reproach to
Chriftianity, that men of this ftamp are
not to be gained over to it ?

Page 616. The great philofophers,
by *their language or their filence, equally
difcover their contempt for the growing
fect* of Chriftianity, *which could not
produce a fingle argument that could en-
gage the attention of men of fenfe and
learning.*—What! Has Mr. Gibbon, indeed, found our religion deferving of
fuch a cenfure as this ! Has not he himfelf made the purity and power of its
precepts, one great caufe of its fuccefs?
And is not this, too, that genuine, divine

vine revelation, which, in his own words, deserves all esteem and veneration ? And has he not but now confessed, that there were some men of sense and learning among the Christians ? And how, then, can he talk with such condemnation of them, and praise of those philosophers, who, in opposition to this religion, persevered in, and defended, such a one as their Paganism was ?

Very deep, indeed, must this gentleman's prejudice be, when it could hinder him from seeing that he must expose himself by such an attack: for when we have the Gospel and its proofs before us, it is of no consequence to us what others have thought of these matters. Will Mr. Gibbon, indeed, set up authority above reason and truth ?—

P   But

But what were thofe philofophers, upon whofe conduct Mr. Gibbon, in thus feverely condemning the Chriftian writers, lays fuch an extraordinary ftrefs? I fhall, fhortly, but with the greateft integrity and juftice, fhew. Till Chriftianity had made a confiderable progrefs, they, for the moft part, rejected a future life, but all of them denied any retribution in it. Their religion was only regarded in order to obtain the good things of this world, and had nothing in it of morality or virtue, but abundance of immorality and wickednefs. The end of man, and his chief happinefs, was totally miftaken by them all: and, bebefides a moft unreasonable attachment to their feveral and contradictory fects, which they thought themfelves bound to follow and maintain, the principles

of

of almost all of them were founded
upon dogmas, not only unfavourable,
but most adverse to Christianity ; and
we know, that every one of them allowed of several vices which true religion abhors and rejects. I need not
enlarge upon this matter ; Mr. Gibbon
must be conscious of it ; I will only
hint at a few particulars.

Plato, in his Republic, recommends a
community of wives, and would have
those men, who had done most service to
the public, allowed a greater liberty in
this way. Socrates himself was infamous for that vice which drew down fire
from heaven upon Sodom and Gomor-
rah ; and the philosophers were so com-
monly addicted to it, that no man, who
had a regard to the purity of his son,

P 2   dared

dared to commit him to their tuition.
How juft, therefore, is the character
given of them by St. Paul, Rom. firft
chap. that *pretending to be wife, they
became fools*, and abandoned themfelves
to the moft fhameful and abominable
vices ! It was a known matter among
themfelves, that their practice, and their
reafoning about virtue, were totally different.—Are thefe, then, the men, upon
whofe opinion we are to reject Chriftianity !—reject the pureft religion which
the world ever faw, and throw ourfelves
back, it may be, into Heathenifm, with
all its abominations ;—deftroy the moft
perfect fyftem of morality, take away
all incitements to virtue, and difcourage-
ment from vice ?—leave no hope of
futurity, or, if there fhould be fuch,
no poffibility of our being happy in it !
                                    Are

Are thefe the men, upon whofe virtue
and integrity we are fo entirely to depend, as, upon their account, to do
ourfelves all thefe deftructive and irrepa-
rable mifchiefs !

Befides, I am to obferve, that thefe
men could relifh nothing but reafon,
the very pride of filly reafon ; and that
it was one main end of the Gofpel to
deftroy this very foolifh and criminal
prefumption, when applied to religion.
It was (befides the teaching us fuch a
purity of life, as might fit us for the
happinefs of heaven) to open the One
Infinite Nature to man, and to do the
higheft honour to it ; and therefore con-
fifted, not of a revelation which could
be reafoned on by man, or any creature,
but of fuch as could only be made
known

known by the Creator himſelf, and proved by the diſplay of his own almighty
power; that is, by controuling that
courſe of nature which he has eſtabliſhed, and which could be done by
his own hand alone; as, alſo, by his
predicting, ſome hundreds, I might
have ſaid thouſands, of years, before
the completion, many contingent events,
which ſhould, in their due time, come
to paſs :—a knowledge this, which no
creature could have, and which ſome
of our *reaſoners* will not allow to be
poſſible even to God himſelf. This revelation was to be the power of God,
and the wiſdom of God; that is, the
exertion of theſe attributes in the higheſt
degree: and was to regard the whole
world, and the government of it, in a manner moſt conducive to its happineſs, even
from

from the creation to the confummation of all things; and muft, therefore, be as fuperior to the faculties of men or angels, as the heavens are above the earth. No wonder, then, that it fhould be defpifed by thofe felf-opinionated men, who imagined all reafon confined to themfelves, but, in truth, never had any proper ideas about religious matters. It neither came, nor was proved, in the way that they wifhed; and, therefore, it was foolifhnefs to them. But St. Paul's affertion will ever remain true, that the foolifhnefs of God is wifer than men; and fo it has remarkably proved in this inftance. As to the underftanding and knowledge of the primitive Chriftian writers, let their works, ftill extant, fpeak for them. The general opinion of the world has hitherto been moft highly in their favour; and who-

ever

ever will read them with any impartiality, will, I believe, entertain the same
sentiments.

Page 617. Mr. Gibbon doubts whether the philosophers perused the Apologies of the Christians for themselves
and their religion. Possibly, they did
not ; but this should not be said by any
man who has a regard for their character : for what reasoners, or respecters
of religion, must they be, who could be
so well satisfied with Heathenism, as to
refuse even to hear any thing that could
be said in opposition to it! He laments,
also, that the Christian *cause was not de-*
fended by abler advocates ; they expose,
with superfluous wit and eloquence, the
extravagance of polytheism, and interest
our compassion by displaying the inno-
cence and sufferings of their injured bre-
thren.

thren.—But how was this fuperfluous, when the philofophers ftill perfevered in the defence of this religion, and the people ftill went on in the cruel perfecution of the Chriftians ?

But they infift much more ftrongly on the predictions which announced, than on the miracles which accompanied, the appearance of the Meffiah.—We ought, at this great diftance of time, to be very cautious how we condemn the method of defence ufed by the primitive Chriftians. We have Origen's book againft Celfus, who, in regard to his own reputation, to his religion, and to the authority by which he is fo often controuled, and hindered from running into allegory, we may be fure, has given us a juft ftate of this philofopher's controverfy : and now I afk Mr. Gibbon,

bon, who has certainly read this work, whether he thinks the arguments of Celsus strong or well-chosen? I will answer for him, that he does not. And yet the Christians, if they would at all reply, must answer such reasonings as these. They, who had been bred up Heathens themselves, and lived among them, and were intimately acquainted with their religion and philosophy, must be much better judges than any of us can be, what the best methods were with which to defend themselves, and to persuade others; and it might have been folly in them to have recourse to such as may now seem to us most fitting and powerful for their purpose. In this instance, however, we can effectually vindicate them.

Those philosophers had the Scriptures
before

before them, which contained an authentic account of many and moft ftupendous miracles having been wrought
by Chrift and his Apoftles, which account, it appears, the Heathens themfelves did not contradiƈt ; and, if thefe
could not convince them, how much
lefs the fewer and leffer that were performed in the church afterwards. But
as all thefe were by the Heathens attributed to magick, and their own gods
were prefumed to perform the like, it
was manifeftly improper for the Chriftians to reft their principal defence upon
a proof of this kind. There was, however, one of them, which was proper,
and this I find infifted upon by Athenagoras, Theophilus, Tertullian, Minu-
tius, Felix, Cyprian, and Origen, and,
probably, by many others ; and this
is the power, which Tertullian fo ftrongly

ly infifted upon, of the Chriftians making the dæmons confefs whom the Heathens worfhipped—that they were dæmons, and not gods. And this very
reafon is given by Origen, in his defence of Chriftianity. He affirms, that
fome remarkable footfteps of this miraculous power, for the confirmation of
the truth of Chriftianity, did remain to
his days; that the church was appointed to deftroy the power of infernal dæmons; that it was abfurd to fuppofe
the Apoftles did no miracles at all, but
relied on their doctrines only; and that
there were fome remnants of this power
to difpoffefs dæmons ftill preferved a-
mong them—If he fhould relate miracles of his own knowledge, it would
furnifh the infidels with a fubject of
laughter, who would be ready to fuf-
pect the Chriftians, as the Chriftians
did

did them, of inventing fictions to support a bad caufe; but he calls God to
witnefs, that in him it was only, by a
proper evidence, to maintain Chriftianity's divine origin.—Thus fpeaks the
great Origen.

But prophecies were much more convincing to the Heathens. The particulars of our Saviour's life and actions
are ftrongly infifted upon by the Chriftian advocates; and the exact eventual
completion of the predictions thereof,
fo many hundred years after they had
been made, was fo full a proof in be-
half of Chriftianity, as left no way to
evade it, but by a denial of their anti-
quity, which, as maintained by Chrift's
greateft enemies, the Jews, could not
be difcredited without a moft manifeft
abfurdity; yet even this abfurdity, great

as

as it was, we find some of them driven
to, affirming the prophecies to be written after the accomplishment of the facts.

What the books of Orpheus, Hermes,
and the Sibyls were, neither I nor
Mr. Gibbon know; but that the latter
(which only is here of importance) were
not a Christian forgery, is unquestionably certain, because they were quoted by
Virgil, and formed a material part of
Christ's character, some years before
he was born: and Athenagoras shews,
that Plato cited them more than 300
years before Christ, to prove their gods
to be deified men. The learned Prideaux has a long dissertation upon this
matter, and concludes, not that they
were Christian forgeries, but that there
were some interpolations made in them
by the Christians; which was very
foolishly

foolifhly done by them, for they thereby rendered thefe books ufelefs to the
caufe they were intended to fupport.
But even this cannot be allowed to that
very learned and honeft man, whofe defire of impartiality has, in this inftance,
carried him a great deal too far.

There were too many of the Sibylline books, and in too many hands, to
have been all corrupted by the Chriftians; nor was it poffible, when the
Heathens had all power in their hands,
for the Chriftians to quote thefe interpolations, without being confuted and
expofed by their enemies, and this to
the ruin of their religion. And that
the reader may have entire fatisfaction
in this matter, I will here fubjoin Mr.
Reeves's note upon it, in his tranflation
of Juftin Martyr's firft Apology.

" The

"The great objection againſt the Sibylline oracles, is, that they ſo plainly
and expreſsly foretel Chriſt to the Heathen world; as plainly as (or more ſo
than) the prophets to the Jews. But
was not Chriſt as manifeſtly foretold by
Balaam the Aramitick Sorcerer, as by
the prophet Iſaiah? Did not Job, who
was not of Iſrael, ſpeak of the great ar-
ticle of the reſurrection? Did not Da-
niel, in his captivity, communicate his
prophecies to the Gentiles, as well as
to the Jews? And was not a prophet
ſent to Jeroboam, an Iſraelite indeed
by birth, but a Pagan by religion. All
which evidently prove, that God never
delivered himſelf more plainly by his
prophets, than when the occaſion re-
ſpected the Gentiles, and not the Jews.
And this likewiſe proves what Clemens
Alexandrinus tells us, 6 Stro. p. 270,
That,

That, as God raiſed up prophets among the Jews, to bring them to ſalvation, " ſic & ſelectiſſimum quemque a Paganis ſervare voluiſſe, prophetas ipſis proprios propria ipſorum dialecto excitando ;" and to theſe Sibyls, Juſtin Martyr, Clemens, Origen, Euſebius, Lactantius, ſent the Heathens for the truth of Chriſtianity, and laid ſo great a ſtreſs upon them as to be called Sibylliſts. But now, had all theſe been forgeries, (not to mention the baſeneſs of a pious fraud, abominated by the firſt Chriſtians,) they never would have been ſo ſillily impudent, as to have appealed to them before the Emperors, and before the world; and Origen never could have challenged Celſus, or any of the Heathens, to give a conſiderable inſtance where theſe books were interpolated by the Chriſtians, which, no doubt, they would have triumphantly

·umphantly done, had there been such in-
terpolation to produce. Moreover, it is
certain, that, in Cicero's time, the Sibylline prophecies were so interpreted
by some in favour of Cæsar, as to pre-
dict a monarchy. Divi. lib. 2, " Eum
quemque revera Regem," &c. *That, if
we would be safe, we should acknowledge
him for a king who really was so*; which
interpretation, Cicero, after Cæsar's
death, was so much offended with, that
he quarrels with the oracles and their
interpreters : " Quamobrem Sibyllam
quidem sepositam," &c. *Wherefore, let
us shut up the Sibyl, and keep her close,
that, according to the decree of our an-
cestors, her verses may not be read without the express command of the Senate.*
And then he adds, "Cum Antistitibus,"
&c. *Let us also deal with the Quinde-
cemviri, and the interpreters of these
Sibylline*

Sibylline books, that they would rather produce any thing out of them than a king. And in the eclogue of Virgil, " Ultima Cumæi venit," &c. written about the beginning of the reign of Herod the Great, and flatteringly applied to Pollio's son, Salonius, such a golden age, and renovation of all things, are spoken of, as cannot be fulfilled in the reign of any earthly king, and in a strain prophetick. The same year that Pompey took Jerusalem, one of the Sibyl oracles made a great noise, that Nature was about to bring forth a king to the Romans: and Suetonius, in the Life of Augustus, saith, that this so terrified the Senate, that they made a decree, that none born that year should be educated; and that those, whose wives were with child, applied the prophecy to themselves. And Appian, Plu-

Q 2   tarch,

tarch, Salluft, and Cicero, all concur in
faying, that it was this prophecy of the
Sibyls which ftirred up Cornelius Len-
tulus at that time, upon the falfe hope
that he was the man defigned for the
king of the Romans. The words of
Suetonius in the Life of Vefpafian are
very remarkable : " Percrebuerat Ori-
ente toto vetus & conftans opinio, effe
in Fatis, ut eo tempore Judea profecti
rerum potirentur." And to the fame
purpofe are thofe of Tacitus : Hift. lib. 5,
" Pluribus perfuafio inerat, antiquis Sa-
cerdotum libris contineri, eo ipfo tempore fore, ut valeret Oriens, profectique
Judea rerum potirentur."

" Now, what I look upon as the moft
probable account of thefe exprefs prophecies concerning Chrift, I mean, as
to the manner of their becoming fo rife
among

among the Heathens, is this :—The Jews, in their difperfions, took all occafions to fpeak the moft magnificent things of their expected Meffiah ; and the prophecies concerning his glory, by the more than ordinary grace of God, fhone brighter and clearer upon their minds during their captivity, and afforded the greateft fupport to them under their exile ; and on thefe occafions it was, I believe, that the Jewifh oracles came to be admitted into the Sibylline books laid up in the Capitol. The books of the Sibyls were of two kinds; thofe bought by Tarquin, and burnt with the Capitol in the time of Sylla, we find from Livy, were full of nothing but idolatry and fuperftition : but after the re-building of the Capitol, there were others brought from Erythræ, by the three ambaffadors deputed for that purpofe ;

pose ; and afterwards others were sent
by Augustus upon the same design, as
we are informed by Tacitus, Ann. c. 6:
" Quæsitus Samo, Ilio, Erythris, per A-
fricam etiam & Siciliam & Italicas co-
lonias, Carminibus Sibyllæ, datum Sa-
cerdotibus negotium, quantum humana
ope potuissent vera discernere." And to
the same purpose Suetonius, Aug. cap. 31.
Now, who can doubt but in this search
after the Sibylline oracles many of the
Jewish prophecies were picked up (especially those famous ones concerning
their new king), and carried with the
rest to Rome : for, after the first were
burnt with the Capitol, who could pos-
possibly distinguish the one from the
other ? And, therefore, Tacitus cautiously adds, in the fore-cited passage,
" quantum humana ope potuissent."

Thus.

Thus argues the learned Mr. Reeves; and now, Dean Prideaux's miſtake, and Mr. Gibbon's too great readineſs to a-buſe the Chriſtians, muſt be manifeſt to every reader.

The aſſertion of inattention paid by the Heathens to the miracles of Chriſt and his Apoſtles, is founded upon a great miſtake. All the miracles of our Saviour were performed among the Jews, a very few in the adjoining Heathen nations excepted ; and what were done among the Heathens in general by the Apoſtles, we know not, except a ſmall number performed by St. Paul to con-firm his preaching. Neither Seneca nor Pliny might ever have ſeen one of them ; nor is it probable that they did. To people prejudiced beyond convic-tion they were never ſhewn ; and that

All-

All-wife Being who was to work them, knew before-hand when they would be ufelefs. Or thefe very people might have feen and neglected them, or not have chofen to fpeak any thing of them: and unlefs they had been converted by them, it is certain that they would not. We are now too well acquainted with the character of *philofophers,* to expect fuch a felf-denying fairnefs and candour from any of them. The fpiteful mif-reprefentations which they give of Chrif-tianity, when they at all fpeak of it, warrants this affertion. But the defen-ders of the primitive Chriftian miracles, againft Dr. Middleton, have fhewn that there was not that dead filence of the Heathens about them which Mr. Gib-bon afferts : they are often mentioned by them, though only to be ridiculed and condemned as magick.

The

The darkness of our Saviour's cruci-
fixion might have been confined to the
land of Judea, and it is now generally
thought to have been so. But that Phle-
gan's teftimony is by us wifely given
up, I know not : Dr. Chapman's differ-
tation upon this fubject, at leaft, fhews
the probability to be on the other fide ;
and, from Origen's quoting it, it is
plain to be of a very ancient ftanding.
—The anfwer given in Dr. Watfon's
book, to the reprefentation here made
of Pliny, fhews it to be a great mif-
.take.

As to Mr. Gibbon's 16th Chapter,
it contains matter fo much lefs affecting
Chriftianity, and what is offenfive in it
is fo particularly confuted by much abler
pens than mine, that I fhall fay nothing
to it.   But here I will congratulate my
R   Chriftian

Chriſtian reader upon the certainty and
ſtrength of his holy faith ; for very
certain and well-founded muſt it indeed
be, when it can withſtand, and without any the leaſt injury to itſelf, the
fierceſt attacks that Mr. Gibbon, with
all his genius and learning, all his deep
prejudices and eagerneſs, could make
to deſtroy it. But it is truly founded
upon a rock, and will remain unſhaken
among us ſo long as we ſhall retain any
juſt ſenſe of the dignity of the nature
of rational and moral man above that
of the irrational and immoral brute,
and are capable of any proſperity in
this world, or happineſs in that which
is to come.

And now I might conclude, but that
I think it firſt neceſſary to warn the
Chriſtian reader againſt being frightened
from

from his religion, by the horrid picture
which he will hereafter find to be drawn
by Mr. Gibbon, and juftly too, in his
hiftory of the next and the two following centuries, when the furious diffentions, animofities, perfecutions, and cruelty of the Chriftians againft each other,
and when the luxury, pride, ambition,
turbulence, of their great and powerful
clergy, will prefent a horrid fcene to his
view ;—very difhonourable, indeed, to
the actors themfelves, but not really
hurtful to their religion ; for, both by
its moft pofitive precepts, and by the
whole tenor of its doctrines, it is the
fartheft removed from, it is the moft
adverfe to, this abominable deftructive
fpirit. But as long as men are men,
and Satan is permitted to range abroad
in the world, there will be fuch things
in it ; and efpecially concerning that
which

which, of all others, deſerves the greateſt
eſteem, and is moſt worthy to be preſerved and contended for, Chriſtianity.

Phil. v. 12, " For we wreſtle not
againſt fleſh and blood, but againſt
principalities, againſt powers, againſt
the rulers of the darkneſs of this world,
againſt ſpiritual wickedneſs (margin,
wicked ſpirits) in high places."

THE END.